CW00481405

GENESIS

GOD'S CREATIVE CALL

CHARLES &
ANNE HUMMEL

26 STUDIES
FOR INDIVIDUALS
OR GROUPS

ivp

Life
Builder
Study

INTER-VARSITY PRESS
36 Causton Street, London SW1P 4ST, England
Email: ivp@ivpbooks.com
Website: www.ivpbooks.com

Originally published in the United States of America in the LifeGuide® Bible Studies series
in 1985 by InterVarsity Press, Downers Grove, Illinois
Second edition published 2000
First published in Great Britain by Scripture Union in 2000
Second UK edition published 2004
This edition published in Great Britain by Inter-Varsity Press 2021

British Library Cataloguing-in-Publication Data
A catalogue record for this book is available from the British Library.

ISBN: 978–1–78359–875–5
eBook ISBN: 978–1–78506–429–6

Printed in Great Britain by Ashford Colour Press Ltd, Gosport, Hampshire

Produced on paper from sustainable sources.

Inter-Varsity Press publishes Christian books that are true to the Bible and that communicate the gospel, develop discipleship and strengthen the church for its mission in the world.

IVP originated within the Inter-Varsity Fellowship, now the Universities and Colleges Christian Fellowship, a student movement connecting Christian Unions in universities and colleges throughout Great Britain, and a member movement of the International Fellowship of Evangelical Students. Website: www.uccf.org.uk. That historic association is maintained, and all senior IVP staff and committee members subscribe to the UCCF Basis of Faith.

Contents

PART 3: JOSEPH—THE MIGRATION TO EGYPT
GENESIS 37—50

Getting the Most Out of *Genesis*

We all look back and wonder about beginnings. Children are fascinated with stories of their birth and babyhood. Families trace their genealogies. Nations write histories. Pressures of the present and hopes for the future take on new meaning when we know more about how it all began.

Genesis is a book of beginnings: the origin of the universe, birth of the human race, founding of the Hebrew nation. Yet this book is more than a record of origins. It lays the foundation for great themes prominent in the Old and New Testaments.

Here we learn about God, humanity and nature in their mutual relationships. The Creator and Controller of the universe reveals himself as the Lord and Judge of history, which has a purpose and goal. Doctrines of covenant, grace and redemption permeate the story of God's actions to overcome the consequences of sin and evil. All trace their origins to this remarkable book.

We should not be surprised that Genesis, more than any other part of the Bible, has been the scene of historical, literary, theological and scientific battles. Some of these conflicts have made their way out of church and seminary into our schools and courts. Since much controversy is fueled by misinformation and secondhand opinion, we need to find out for ourselves what the biblical text teaches and, equally important, what it does *not* teach.

The purpose of this guide is to help you learn the meaning of Genesis for those who first heard it, then for us today. You may be surprised to discover how clear it is when we let the author tell the message in his own way—without importing questions he never intended to ask, much less answer.

Much of Genesis consists of stories—the history of individuals, families, tribes and nations. You will find that some of their experiences mirror your own, reflecting the way God wants to lead you into new ways of knowing and serving him. We wish you well in your search.

Historical Context

Genesis is the first of five books called the Pentateuch. The New Testament attributes these writings to Moses. During the last century critics have questioned the Mosaic authorship of the Pentateuch. Nevertheless, a strong case can be made for the traditional view that Moses wrote most of the Pentateuch, even though he may have used existing sources for Genesis. At any rate, we will assume that the message of Genesis was given to Israel during the years in the wilderness around 1250 B.C. Therefore, we need to know something of Israel's cultural and religious situation in order to understand what the author intends to teach.

For about 400 years the Hebrews had languished in Egypt far from the land promised to Abraham. Those centuries took a spiritual as well as a physical toll. The Hebrews had no scriptures, only some oral patriarchal traditions. Except for a few midwives, the fear of the Lord had been supplanted by cultic worship of the gods of other nations. Even after they were delivered from slavery and led toward Canaan, the people apparently had little knowledge of the God of their forefather Abraham.

When the Hebrews arrived at Mount Sinai, their worldview and lifestyle differed little from that of neighboring nations. Their culture was essentially pagan. Now God was calling them to keep his covenant, to become a "kingdom of priests and a holy nation" (Exodus 19:6). Although the people assented enthusiastically, their "yes" was just the beginning of a long, painful process by which God would create a new culture to fulfill their vocation.

Moses faced a formidable task. The people needed a radically different theology to know God and his purpose in history, another lifestyle for moral and ethical living, and a new cosmology to reorient their attitudes toward the natural world. The five books of Moses were designed to make the Hebrews a people of God through this new, divinely instituted culture. For that reason, the Pentateuch provides strong anti-pagan teaching to help God's people make a clean break with the past and learn to look at all of life from his point of view.

The Role of Genesis

This first book opens with an account of the beginning of the universe that lays the foundation for Israel's new view of the world. The narrative strikes hard not only at the nature gods worshiped by their pagan neighbors but also at an array of false philosophies which have led large sections of the human race astray in every century.

> Genesis 1 affirms a radical and comprehensive monotheism versus every kind of false religion (polytheism, idolatry, animism, pantheism and syncretism); superstition (astrology and magic); and philosophy (materialism, ethical dualism, naturalism and nihilism). That is a remarkable achievement for so short an account (about 900 words) written in everyday language and understood by people in a variety of cultures for more than three thousand years. (Charles Hummel, *The Galileo Connection* [Downers Grove, Ill.: InterVarsity Press, 1986], pp. 216-17)

The creation of the world culminates in God's forming a man and woman. But they soon rebel against their Creator and plunge humanity into sin with its devastating consequences. From then on Genesis recounts the drama of God's mighty acts of judgment and mercy as his redemptive purpose unfolds. Our study of Genesis is divided into three main parts:

1. Creation and Primeval History, chapters 1—11
2. Abraham, Isaac and Jacob: The Emergence of Israel, chapters 12—36
3. Joseph: The Migration to Egypt, chapters 37—50

Throughout these narratives, a central and organizing theme is the "call of God." His creative word initially calls the whole creation into being. God then calls into existence a covenant community to be his special people. Genesis and the whole Old Testament look forward to his new creation and covenant in Jesus Christ, into whose fellowship we also are called.

Suggestions for Individual Study

1. As you begin each study, pray that God will speak to you through his Word.

2. Read the introduction to the study and respond to the personal reflection question or exercise. This is designed to help you focus on God and on the theme of the study.

3. Each study deals with a particular passage—so that you can delve into the author's meaning in that context. Read and reread the passage to be studied. If you are studying a book, it will be helpful to read through the entire book prior to the first study. The questions are written using the language of the New International Version, so you may wish to use that version of the Bible. The New Revised Standard Version is also recommended.

4. This is an inductive Bible study, designed to help you discover for yourself what Scripture is saying. The study includes three types of questions. *Observation* questions ask about the basic facts: who, what, when, where and how. *Interpretation* questions delve into the meaning of the passage. *Application* questions help you discover the implications of the text for growing in Christ. These three keys unlock the treasures of Scripture.

Write your answers to the questions in the spaces provided or in a personal journal. Writing can bring clarity and deeper understanding of yourself and of God's Word.

5. It might be good to have a Bible dictionary handy. Use it to look up any unfamiliar words, names or places.

6. Use the prayer suggestion to guide you in thanking God for what you have learned and to pray about the applications that have come to mind.

7. You may want to go on to the suggestion under "Now or Later," or you may want to use that idea for your next study.

Suggestions for Members of a Group Study

1. Come to the study prepared. Follow the suggestions for individual study mentioned above. You will find that careful preparation will greatly enrich your time spent in group discussion.

2. Be willing to participate in the discussion. The leader of your group will not be lecturing. Instead, he or she will be encouraging the members of the group to discuss what they have learned. The leader will be asking the questions that are found in this guide.

3. Stick to the topic being discussed. Your answers should be based on the verses which are the focus of the discussion and not on outside authorities such as commentaries or speakers. These studies focus on a particular passage of Scripture. Only rarely should you refer to other portions of the Bible. This allows for everyone to participate in in-depth study on equal ground.

4. Be sensitive to the other members of the group. Listen attentively when they describe what they have learned. You may be surprised by their insights! Each question assumes a variety of answers. Many questions do not have "right" answers, particularly questions that aim at meaning or application. Instead the questions push us to explore the passage more thoroughly.

When possible, link what you say to the comments of others. Also, be affirming whenever you can. This will encourage some of the more hesitant members of the group to participate.

5. Be careful not to dominate the discussion. We are sometimes so eager to express our thoughts that we leave too little opportunity for others to respond. By all means participate! But allow others to also.

6. Expect God to teach you through the passage being discussed and through the other members of the group. Pray that you will have an enjoyable and profitable time together, but also that as a result of the study you will find ways that you can take action individually and/or as a group.

7. Remember that anything said in the group is considered confidential and should not be discussed outside the group unless specific permission is given to do so.

8. If you are the group leader, you will find additional suggestions at the back of the guide.

1

The Creation: Our Special Place in the World

Genesis 1:1—2:3

Have you ever been involved in a discussion about creation? Do you wonder why it generates so much controversy? This study will help you understand the author's original purpose and what it can mean for us today.

GROUP DISCUSSION. Briefly tell about the most beautiful place you have ever seen. How has that experience increased your appreciation for the Creator?

PERSONAL REFLECTION. Spend some time praising God for his creation.

Like other books in the Bible, Genesis 1 describes natural events in popular and nontechnical language. It reports them as they appear to the average person without explaining exactly *how* they take place. The emphasis is on the who and why, the Creator and his purposes in creation. *Read Genesis 1:1—2:3.*

1. As the passage is read, what words and phrases do you find repeated?

2. Describe in your own words how the earth appears at the outset.

3. In what ways do God's creative commands during the first three days add form to the formless earth (1:3-13)?

4. How do God's commands during the next three days add fullness to the empty earth (1:14-25)?

5. In what ways does God view his creation as being good (1:4, 10, 12, 18, 21, 25)?

6. The creation account reveals that God brings order, beauty and harmony out of an originally chaotic situation. In what areas do you need to trust God to produce these qualities in your life?

7. What does it mean to be made in the image of God (1:26-27)?

8. What special commands and provisions does God give to the man and woman in his creation (1:28-31)?

9. How is the seventh day uniquely different from the other six (2:1-3)?

10. In our culture how can we experience the "rest" described here?

11. In light of what you have learned about God in this study, how can you reflect his image in practical ways during the next seven days?

Ask God to continue to teach you what it means to live as one made in his image.

Now or Later

List the various kinds of human creativity—including your own—that reflect God's creativity. What does this reveal to you about God?

2

Adam & Eve: Life as God Intended It

Genesis 2:4-25

For of all sad words of tongue or pen,
The saddest are these: "It might have been!"

These words take on special meaning when we look at life as the Creator originally intended it.

GROUP DISCUSSION. In what ways have we failed to be good stewards of God's earth?

PERSONAL REFLECTION. In your own life, what "might have been" situations do you recall?

Genesis 2 moves from the earth at large to the smaller stage of "a garden of the east." Here there is a colorful picture of plant and animal life. This narrative is different from the first in both content and style. Yet it continues to be historical rather than parable or myth. Its focus is on Adam and Eve. This record is a basis for understanding who we were meant to be in relation to God, nature and each other. *Read Genesis 2:4-25.*

1. In verses 4-6 how is the condition of the earth different from the picture we saw in the first chapter?

2. How is the creation of the man in verse 7 unique in comparison with the rest of God's creation?

3. What more do we learn about God's creativity from verses 8-14?

4. Note the responsibility and instructions given to Adam in verses 15-17. What do they reveal about the life God originally intended for us?

5. What does verse 18 show about the depth of God's concern for his human creation?

6. Note the social dimension of being created in the image of God. What implications does this have for our relationship with others?

7. In verses 19-20 how is the man's relationship to the beasts and the birds demonstrated?

8. What do we learn about the woman from this account of her creation in verses 20-23?

_____

9. How does Adam's statement in verse 23 reflect his appreciation of his new partner?

_____

10. In your own words explain what you think verse 24 teaches about marriage.

_____

11. What light does verse 25 throw on the relationship between the man and the woman?

_____

12. How does this passage help you understand who you were created to be?

Pray for guidance in strengthening a relationship that has been weakened.

Now or Later

Bring any "might have been" situations in your life to the Lord for his healing.

3

The First Sin:
How Can We
Deal with Temptation?

Genesis 3

If God is good and powerful, why does he allow so much evil and pain? Although the Bible doesn't answer this question directly, it shows how sin and its consequences entered the world.

GROUP DISCUSSION. How would you explain the difference between temptation and sin?

PERSONAL REFLECTION. What areas of temptation cause you the greatest concern?

The last chapter left Adam and Eve at peace with God, themselves and the natural world over which they had been given stewardship. They were free to eat any fruit of the garden—with one exception. In this chapter we will see how they handled that test and what lessons we can learn from their experience. *Read Genesis 3.*

1. As you heard the drama unfold, what impressed you about the serpent's strategy and his representation of God's command?

2. What do you think of Eve's response (vv. 2-3)?

3. In what ways do we tend to make God's commands more restrictive than he intends?

How does this affect our view of his requirements?

4. As the serpent interprets God's instructions, what does he promise (vv. 4-5)?

5. From your experience how does Satan try to deceive us about the consequences and supposed benefits of sin?

6. How have the serpent's words distorted Eve's thinking (v. 6), and what action does she take as a result?

7. In verses 7-13 describe the effect of Adam and Eve's disobedience on their attitude toward themselves and God.

8. What mistakes do Adam and Eve make?

Have any of these kinds of mistakes led you to disobey God?

9. Describe in your own words the punishments the Lord pronounces on the serpent, the woman and the man (vv. 14-19).

10. In what ways is life now different from God's original plan?

11. How does God finally end this era in Eden?

What shows his continuing concern for Adam and Eve (vv. 21-24)?

12. What lessons have you learned in this study that can help you recognize and resist a temptation you are facing?

Pray for the Lord's strength to take this action.

Now or Later

Reread the three divine punishments and consider what relevance they may have for you today.

4

Cain & Abel: Attitudes & Reactions to Sin

Genesis 4—5

A Lutheran bishop who lived in East Germany suffered fierce persecution by the Nazis and then the Communists. He declared, "When God is not God, man is not man." He had seen how rejection of divine authority leads to inhuman actions. We now look at this principle at work in the newly created human family.

GROUP DISCUSSION. What situation in your life shows a link between people's view of God and their treatment of others?

PERSONAL REFLECTION. Think of a situation in which a wrong attitude on your part led to a sinful action. Present it to God prayerfully before you begin your study.

Read Genesis 4.

1. What impresses you about Cain and Abel?

2. In verses 1-5 what do we learn about the two brothers and their offerings?

3. How do verses 6-8 describe God's response to Cain and Cain's reaction?

4. Cain is told that sin is crouching at the door and he must master it. What happens when we refuse to admit that we are on the wrong track?

5. What resources do we have to overcome sin?

6. In verses 9-10 how does the exchange between God and Cain strike you?

7. Describe in your own words God's judgment on Cain and his reaction (vv. 11-14).

8. How does God protect Cain (vv. 15-16)?

In what way does seeing God's protection of Cain in the midst of punishment give us encouragement?

_____

9. In verses 17-26 life goes on; describe Lamech's attitude and action.

_____

10. The lifestyle of Cain's family is a picture of humanity: technical progress matched by moral decline. How do you see this reality in our own civilization?

_____

11. What gives an element of hope in the midst of this sad story (vv. 25-26)?

_____

12. How does the chapter help you understand the characteristics and consequences of sin?

Ask the Lord to help you recognize his voice urging you to stay on the track of his will.

Now or Later

Scan chapter 5 to trace the line from Seth to Noah—the subject of the next study.

5

The Flood:
Two Lifestyles &
Their Results

Genesis 6—7

Does it really make much difference how we live? Each day's headline news reminds us that good so often goes unrewarded while evil persists without punishment.

GROUP DISCUSSION. What prevalent evils do you see growing and infecting our current society?

PERSONAL REFLECTION. How do you live in a sinful world without being drawn into it or isolating yourself and losing contact?

Although these chapters don't answer all our questions about the struggle with evil, they show how eventually God's justice and judgment can become evident. *Read Genesis 6.*

1. What impresses you about the human condition at Noah's time?

2. What words in verses 5 and 11 emphasize the extent of wickedness?

3. In what way has God's attitude toward the creation changed since the beginning (vv. 1:1-31; 6:6-7, 11-13, 17)?

4. How do current newspaper and TV headlines illustrate some ways our civilization resembles Noah's?

5. How is Noah different from his contemporaries (6:5-12)?

6. What do you think God's plans and provision for Noah's family and the various living creatures show about his continuing concern for his creation (6:13-22)?

7. In verse 18 what is meant by God's establishing a covenant with Noah?

8. *Read Genesis 7.* How do you suppose Noah and his family feel during the long months of building the ark in a very dry land and rounding up the animals (7:1-16)?

9. When have you felt embarrassed in front of others because of your obedience to the Lord?

10. How can you be encouraged and challenged by Noah's example?

11. In verse 16 how does God's action impress you?

12. What details are given about the flood and its results (7:17-24)?

13. The events of these chapters reveal the grace and justice of God. What aspect of this speaks to you personally?

Pray that God will show how your witness, like Noah's, can be evident in your community.

Now or Later

List areas of evil or injustice in your community. What possible activities would help in defeating them?

6

The Rainbow:
God's Promises
for the Future

Genesis 8:1—9:17

How do you feel when you see the long-awaited fulfillment of one of God's promises? To what extent is your response similar to that of Noah and his family?

GROUP DISCUSSION. If you were onboard the ark, how would you feel from the time God shut the door to about a year later when he said, "Come out on deck"?

PERSONAL REFLECTION. Think of a time when you were called to step out in faith on a risky venture in service to the Lord.

In this study we see how God fulfills his promise to Noah, providing an example for us today. *Read Genesis 8.*

1. How is God's concern for his people expressed in 8:1-5?

2. What initiative does Noah take during this period (8:6-14)?

3. In what way can his example help us understand our responsibility during a period when we are depending on God to work?

4. In 8:15-19 how does God's instruction show his continuing concern for the voyagers?

5. What does Noah's first action after emptying the ark (8:20) reveal about his priorities in what must have been an incredibly busy time?

6. What aspect of Noah's example—obedience, faith, courage, patience—is most meaningful to you in a situation you are facing?

7. How does the Lord respond to Noah's sacrifice (8:21-22)?

8. Why is his promise especially remarkable in view of the continuing sinfulness of human nature?

9. *Read Genesis 9:1-17.* What commission does God give to Noah and his family in 9:1-7?

10. Where do you see differences from the original command to Adam in 1:27-30?

11. In 9:8-17 how is the sign of the rainbow especially appropriate to God's promise?

12. In what ways has God's grace been evident throughout this passage?

13. How have you seen his grace at work in your life?

Spend some time in prayer thanking God for his grace to us who don't deserve it.

Now or Later
Write down some instances of God's grace in answer to your prayer for others in your life.

7

The Tower of Babel: Problems in Family & Society

Genesis 9:18—11:32

Every generation has the problem of disrespect for authority—both divine and human. This attitude continues after the flood in Noah's family, then on a larger scale in society.

GROUP DISCUSSION. Where do you see a breakdown in family relationships reaping a harvest of problems in your community?

PERSONAL REFLECTION. Where do you see a situation in which a character flaw appears to pass from generation to generation?

We have seen that Noah's new commission from God is similar to the one given Adam. Now we see how sin again spreads from father to son in both private and public realms. *Read Genesis 9:18-29.*

---

1. Describe what happens in this brief story of Noah and his sons.

2. How does Ham's conduct dishonor his father?

In what ways does it contrast with the action of his brothers?

3. What are Noah's reactions to the conduct of his sons (9:24-27)?

4. In what ways do you think families today suffer from disrespect of parents?

5. How can we show respect to our parents regardless of their actions toward us?

6. *Read Genesis 11:1-9.* What actions do the people of Babel take and what is their motive (vv. 11:1-4)?

7. How does this project conflict with God's instruction to Noah after the flood?

8. What is the Lord's reaction in 11:5-9?

9. Why do you think all human efforts to achieve world unity fall short of what God desires?

10. As you come to the end of the first eleven chapters of Genesis (which comprise part one of this guide), how have these chapters helped you see God as a God of love, mercy and tender concern as well as a God of justice and judgment?

11. What in this section of study has been most meaningful to you in your understanding of God?

Thank God that he continually reveals himself to us.

Now or Later

Scan Genesis 10, which traces the descendants of Shem, Ham and Japheth. What interesting facts does this chapter reveal about the spread of humanity after the flood? (Note especially 10:5, 8-15, 25.)

Read Genesis 11:10-32. Why do you think the author shifts from writing about all the families of the earth to one family?

8

Abram's Call: Following God into the Unknown

Genesis 12—13

Suppose God asked you to leave all that is familiar—your home, family, friends—and follow him into another part of the country or world. How would you feel as you said goodbye and moved out into a radically different lifestyle?

GROUP DISCUSSION. Tell about an occasion when you believed God was asking you to take a step involving uncertainty or risk.

PERSONAL REFLECTION. What was the reaction of family or friends to a decision you've made to follow the Lord on a new, perhaps risky, path?

In this study we can learn from the example of Abram as he responds to God's call. *Read Genesis 12.*

1. In 12:1-5 what command and promise does the Lord give to Abram?

2. Describe in your own words what is involved for Abram and his family to leave their homes and relatives (12:4-5).

3. What do you think his obedience cost him in personal relationships?

4. What additional promise and encouragement does God give to Abram as he arrives in Canaan and how does he respond (12:6-9)?

5. What guidance or encouragement has God provided to you as you followed his call into an unfamiliar and frightening situation?

6. In verses 10-16 how does Abram's scheming show a lack of faith?

7. How does the Lord save Abram from his own deception (12:17-20)?

8. Describe a time when you took matters into your own hands instead of trusting God's faithfulness. What were the results for you and others involved?

9. *Read Genesis 13.* What problem arises between Abram and Lot in 13:1-7?

10. How does Abram's action here demonstrate a greater confidence in God's promise to take care of him (13:8-13)?

11. What expanded promises does the Lord give to Abram (13:14-17)?

12. Why do you think the Lord chooses this moment to speak to him?

13. How can Abram's experience in these two chapters encourage you to trust your needs more fully to God?

Thank God for the way he has met one of your recent needs.

Now or Later

Write down any fork in the road ahead that may call for you to make a decision of this kind.

9

Conflict & Covenant: Tests of Faith

Genesis 14—15

If you want your faith to increase, don't be surprised or disheartened over difficulties that demand it. Muscles of faith grow strong through training and testing that are sometimes painful.

GROUP DISCUSSION. Recall a situation that motivated you to become involved in a struggle for a just cause of some kind.

PERSONAL REFLECTION. What troubling situation in your life may be an opportunity for strengthening the muscles of your faith?

Abram continues to learn how difficulties grow faith after parting from his nephew Lot. *Read Genesis 14.*

1. In what way does the political and military situation described in 14:1-4 resemble hostilities we see in the world today?

2. Describe the battle and its results for Lot and his family (14:5-12).

3. When he learns of Lot's capture, what strategy does Abram devise (14:13-16)?

4. Who is Melchizedek, and what does he do (14:18-20)?

5. In what way does his blessing help Abram put his victory in proper perspective?

6. Why does Abram react as he does to the generous offer made by the king of Sodom (14:21-24)?

7. What evidence do you find of Abram's growing confidence in God?

8. *Read Genesis 15.* At this point what is Abram's main problem, and how does he propose to solve it (15:2-3)?

9. In what way would the Lord's message renew the patriarch's confidence (15:1, 4-5)?

10. Verse 6 is the first time we read that Abram *believed* the Lord. Explain in your own words what it means that the Lord "credited it [his faith] to him as righteousness."

11. What new promises by the Lord are given in the covenant he now makes (15:7-21)?

12. If you have ever had to wait a long time for God to fulfill a promise, what did you learn in the process about yourself, the Lord and his way of working?

13. God promised to be Abram's shield and very great reward. Picture God speaking those words to you. How does that promise encourage you in an area you are struggling with?

Thank the Lord for circumstances in your life that can help your faith grow.

Now or Later

Create a "lifeline" depicting your Christian life. Draw a line representing your ups and downs with God over the years. How have you seen difficult circumstances lead to growth over time?

10

Ishmael & Isaac: Faith Falters & Is Renewed

Genesis 16—17

Do you ever get tired of waiting for God to act? Do you sometimes wonder whether your faith is simply foolishness? At such times it is tempting to become an activist. "If *God* won't help me, I'll do it *myself*."

GROUP DISCUSSION. How has waiting for God to act caused you to take matters into your own hands?

PERSONAL REFLECTION. What have you learned about God's faithfulness in times of waiting?

Here we find Sarai and Abram frustrated by the passing years without a son. So they devise their own strategy for "fulfilling" God's promise—and reap the consequences. *Read Genesis 16.*

1. It has been ten years since Abram and Sarai entered Canaan. What action does Sarai now suggest (16:1-2)?

2. What do you think this indicates about their trust in God?

3. How can our impatience with God's timetable lead us into unbelief and even disobedience?

4. After Hagar conceives, how do the relationships among the three main characters change (16:3-6)?

5. What action does Hagar take and what does she learn about the Lord in this traumatic experience (16:6-14)?

6. When has a difficult time in your own life helped you gain new insight into God's concern for you?

7. *Ishmael* means "the God who hears." What does that reveal about the outcome in 16:15-16?

8. *Read Genesis 17.* What most impresses you about God's affirmation of his covenant?

9. In 17:1-8 what is significant about the change in the patriarch's name from *Abram* ("exalted father") to *Abraham* ("father of many")?

10. What instruction does God give Abraham as an outward sign of the covenant (17:9-14)?

11. In 17:15-16 what specific promise does God make about Sarai, now to be called *Sarah* ("princess")?

How does Abraham respond in 17:17-18, and why?

12. In 17:19-22 how does God answer Abraham about his future and the future of Isaac and Ishmael?

13. What have you learned about God in this chapter to help you believe his promises in spite of your circumstances?

Thank God that he is God Almighty and always keeps his promises.

Now or Later

Write down what you have learned about God in this chapter to help you believe his promise concerning one area of your life.

11

Sodom & Gomorrah: God's Judgment on Society

Genesis 18—19

Contemporary Christianity has been described as "privately engaging but socially irrelevant." Many of us concern ourselves with only family and church to the neglect of the broader arenas of work and community—the economic, political and social fabric of our society.

GROUP DISCUSSION. In your town, how are churches demonstrating concern for the poor and the disadvantaged?

PERSONAL REFLECTION. What areas of need do you see around you, and how do you think God may want you to become involved?

So far we have seen Abraham involved only in his personal and family concerns. In this passage, however, he broadens his perspective to become involved in the problems of a neighboring city whose lifestyle is the opposite to everything he stands for. Abraham's reaction to the news of impending judgment can help us today concerning responsible Christian action in our postmodern society. *Read Genesis 18.*

1. If you were one of the strangers in 18:1-8, what elements of hospi-

tality in Abraham's welcome would impress you?

2. In 18:9-15 why does Sarah react as she does to the promise of a son?

How might the Lord's response be both a rebuke and an encouragement?

3. Why does the Lord decide to tell Abraham his plans (18:16-19)?

4. In the dialogue that takes place in 18:20-33, what can you learn about Abraham's attitude toward the wicked cities and toward the Lord?

5. How would you describe the Lord's attitude toward the cities and his relationship with Abraham?

6. In what ways can we intercede with God for our city, our state and our country because of its sins?

7. How might this kind of prayer affect our attitudes and actions toward those around us?

8. *Read Genesis 19:1-29.* In 19:1-9 how do the actions of the inhabitants of Sodom help us see why they are under God's judgment?

9. What effects does life in Sodom seem to have had on Lot and his family (19:1-14)?

10. How is the Lord's mercy evident in his treatment of Lot and his family (19:10-22)?

11. Describe how God's judgment works out in Lot's family and in the two cities (19:23-29).

12. Living in the midst of a sinful society, what is a warning for you?

What is an encouragement?

Thank God that he reveals himself to us as he did to Abraham, saying, "Is anything too hard for the Lord?"

Now or Later

Read Genesis 19:30-38. What are the results of Lot's earlier choices in the life of his family?

12

Political & Family Crises: Consequences of Unbelief

Genesis 20—21

Have you ever gotten into trouble because you didn't trust God to take care of you? Did you take matters into your own hands and in the process cut some moral or ethical corner? If so, you have company! The Bible has no plaster saints; it doesn't cover over the sins of its heroes. Even Abraham gave in to his fears and failed to tell the truth in a potentially dangerous situation.

GROUP DISCUSSION. Consider a time when you spoke only a part of the truth when a full answer was called for.

PERSONAL REFLECTION. Recall a situation when it appeared that a "non-Christian" was acting more ethically than a believer.

In the previous study we saw Abraham at his best; here we find him near his worst. But we can learn from Abraham's failures as well as his successes. *Read Genesis 20.*

1. Describe Abraham's action and how God deals with it in 20:1-7.

2. How does God's conversation with Abimelech show his concern even for those who are outside his covenant relationship?

3. From 20:8-10 what are your impressions of Abimelech in his encounter with Abraham?

4. As Abraham tries to explain his way out of his difficulty (20:11-13), what potential consequences does his action have for Sarah, their promised son and Abimelech's family?

5. Think of a situation when your stretching of the truth had serious consequences. What did you learn?

6. As this episode ends, how is Abraham's stature restored (20:14-18)?

7. Seeing the effects of Abraham's fear and lack of trust, what can we learn from this account to help us deal with the ongoing fears we have?

8. *Read Genesis 21.* Describe how Sarah feels in 21:1-7 after waiting so long to bear a child.

9. How can Sarah and Abraham's experience encourage us to be more patient while we wait for prayers to be answered?

10. In 21:8-14 what problem does Abraham face and how is it solved?

11. How does God help and encourage Hagar in her hour of crisis (21:15-21)?

12. What does Abimelech's request show about his attitude toward Abraham (21:22-34)?

13. How can God's grace and faithfulness to the main characters in this account motivate you to trust him the next time you are filled with fear or doubt?

Ask God to help you identify and surrender to him any fear or anxiety that undermines your confidence and trust in him.

Now or Later

Journal about a crucial need you have had that God met in an unusual way—as he did with Hagar.

13

The Sacrifice of Isaac: Ultimate Faith & Obedience

Genesis 22—23

Suppose God asked you to give up someone or something at the very center of your life—a loved one, your home, profession or plans for the future. How would you respond? Sometimes God calls us to follow him in ways that don't make sense to us.

GROUP DISCUSSION. How have you felt when God seems to be calling you to a new course of action that is contrary to guidance he had already given?

PERSONAL REFLECTION. In what family relationship is your obedience to the will of God causing some strain?

In this study we walk with Abraham through a valley of testing in a soul-wracking experience. His example can help us learn how God provides for those who honor him with their trust. *Read Genesis 22.*

---

1. In 22:1-2 what phrases emphasize the importance and difficulty of God's command?

2. Describe some of the thoughts and emotions you would have if you were Abraham.

3. What do the details of the narrative reveal about Abraham's response to this incredibly difficult assignment (22:3-10)?

4. Notice God's words to Abraham in 22:12. Based on Abraham's example what does it mean to "fear" God?

5. How does God's provision in 22:13-14 fulfill the confidence Abraham expresses in 22:5, 8?

6. Describe a time when obedience to God required you to give up someone or something you loved.

How did the Lord provide for you in that difficult time?

7. In verses 15-19 why is it an especially appropriate time for the Lord to reaffirm his promises?

8. *Read Genesis 23.* When Abraham decides to bury Sarah among the Hittites, how do they react to his first request (23:1-6)?

9. How does he then proceed to secure her grave (23:7-16)?

10. Why do you think Abraham persists in his desire to own the burial plot?

11. How was the purchase of her grave a sign of trust that God was going to give them their own land?

12. How can these two chapters encourage us to trust God when we still don't see the answers to our pressing needs?

Pray that God will increase your trust in him as you walk paths of uncertainty.

Now or Later

In what ways do you find yourself identifying with Abraham in this test of faith and obedience?

14

A Wife for Isaac: God's Guidance & Care

Genesis 24:1—25:11

How do you go about discovering God's will in a specific situation? When you think you understand it, do you simply wait or do you work toward its fulfillment? Although the Bible gives no formulas or blueprints, it does illustrate certain principles we can apply.

GROUP DISCUSSION. When you think of God's guidance, what causes you the greatest difficulty?

PERSONAL REFLECTION. Look back on your life to the various ways God has guided you. Take time to thank God for what comes to mind.

In this study Abraham continues to wind up his affairs by arranging for the sure succession of his line. Here we have the fascinating story of the way he went about securing the right wife for his son Isaac. *Read Genesis 24:1-27.*

1. What do you think are Abraham's main concerns when he gives instruction to his servant (24:1-9)?

2. When the servant arrives at his destination, he offers the first prayer for guidance recorded in the Bible. What does he specifically ask of God (24:10-14)?

3. From 24:15-25 describe Rebekah in your own words.

4. What does the servant's prayer in 24:26-27 reveal about his own relationship with God?

5. *Read Genesis 24:28-66.* In 24:28-33 what are your impressions of Laban?

6. How does the servant's account in 24:34-49 reveal his excitement and awe at the Lord's guidance?

7. The servant did not ask for a vision or miraculous event but for guidance through clear signs in natural circumstances. When has God guided you this way?

8. How does Rebekah's family react to these unexpected events, and in what way is she involved in the decision-making (24:50-60)?

9. Describe the return of Rebekah with her servant and what her arrival must have meant to Isaac.

10. How can this account of God's providing a wife for Isaac be an example to us of God's guidance and loving care?

11. *Read Genesis 25:1-11.* What do we learn about Abraham's final years?

12. How would you sum up his life in one sentence?

13. What is the most important lesson you have learned from studying the life of Abraham?

Thank God for the example of Abraham's life, showing both failure and faith.

Now or Later

List all that you have learned from Abraham about his relationship with God and God's covenant with him.

15

Jacob & Esau:
A Family Feud

Genesis 25:12—27:40

Sibling rivalry is prevalent in most families and is part of growing up. It can be contained if dealt with consistently and fairly. But when parents show partiality, this struggle often becomes fatal to family unity.

GROUP DISCUSSION. Within your own family what has been the most difficult sibling relationship for you and why?

PERSONAL REFLECTION. How can you appreciate the blessings and accept the challenges of being in the family where God has put you?

This study opens with the joy of a long-awaited birth. After twenty years Isaac and Rebekah have not just one son but twins. As the boys grow up, parental partiality develops with tragic consequences for family relationships. Yet throughout these events, God works out his sovereign purpose and remains merciful to this special family in spite of their failures. *Read Genesis 25:12-34.*

---

1. In Genesis 25:19-22 what difficulties and tests of faith do Isaac and Rebekah encounter in the birth of their sons?

2. What do we learn about Esau and Jacob from before their birth until they grow up (25:23-28)?

3. What does Esau's attitude toward his birthright reveal about his character (25:29-34)?

4. In what situation are you tempted to give up something of spiritual value to meet an immediate need?

5. *Read Genesis 26:1-11.* How does Isaac follow his father's footsteps in his dealings with Abimelech?

6. In what ways have your parents' strengths and weaknesses affected you, and what can you do about them?

7. *Read Genesis 27:1-40.* Remember we read, "Isaac loved Esau but Rebekah loved Jacob" (25:28). In verses 1-17 how do we see this parental favoritism working destructively within the family?

8. As a parent (or relative or teacher) how can you show equal love and acceptance to children with radically different personalities?

9. Describe how Jacob goes about deceiving his father, and the blessing he receives (vv. 18-29).

10. Put in your own words Esau's reaction and what he was given.

11. As a result of this study what one thing can you do within your own family (or present living situation) to reduce tension and encourage better relationships?

Thank God for the blessing he gives you through your family.

Now or Later

12. Read Genesis 26:12-35. What ongoing problem does Isaac face in 26:12-22?

13. How does Isaac respond to God's promises in 26:24?

14. What effect does Isaac's blessing have on his enemies?

15. Being the recipient of God's blessing did not mean smooth sailing for Isaac. How can his experience encourage us to accept God's way and God's timing?

16

Jacob in Exile: God's Mercy & Justice

Genesis 27:41—30:24

How do you cope with the consequences of sin in your life? What effect does your disobedience to God have on his purposes for you? Jacob's experience can provide answers to these questions.

GROUP DISCUSSION. Describe a family you know with stress and division dividing parents and children.

PERSONAL REFLECTION. How could you help a friend caught in a difficult family situation?

In the last study we saw how parental partiality increased the natural rivalry between Esau and Jacob. As Isaac and Rebekah took sides, the family relationships became strained. In this study they finally fracture with unforeseen consequences. *Read Genesis 27:41—28:9.*

1. When Rebekah hears of Esau's plan to kill Jacob, what strategy does she come up with, and how does she persuade Jacob and Isaac to carry it out (27:41-46)?

2. In what specific ways would Isaac's instructions encourage Jacob as he leaves home and sets out on his long journey (28:1-5)?

3. In 28:6-9 what effect does Isaac's action have on Esau?

4. *Read Genesis 28:10-22.* Describe what happens to Jacob on his first night away from home (28:10-15).

5. From Jacob's response to the dream, what clue do we get about his relationship to God at this point (28:16-22)?

6. A past sin or disobedience to God can leave us with a burden of guilt and a sense of failure. How can Jacob's experience renew our confidence in God's grace?

7. *Read Genesis 29.* What impresses you about Jacob's initial actions and reception in the account of his arrival in Paddan Aram (29:1-14)?

8. In what way does Laban's trickery repay Jacob for deceiving his father (29:15-24)?

9. How is this situation resolved (29:29-30)?

10. What do we learn about Leah from the names she gives her sons (29:31-35)?

11. *Read Genesis 30:1-24.* How would you describe the relationship between the two sisters?

12. How does this traumatic triangle work its hardship on each person involved?

13. Spiritual maturity often comes through suffering. In what difficult situations do you see God now working to strengthen your faith and character?

Spend time thanking God for his care and discipline in your life.

Now or Later

Looking back over your life, in what ways have you experienced growth and deepening of your relationship with God?

17

Jacob Versus Laban: Rivalry & Its Results

After marrying both Leah and Rachel, Jacob was obligated to serve their father for another seven years. Now he wants to return to his homeland with his family. We will see how the rivalry between these two men escalates to the point of open conflict.

GROUP DISCUSSION. Tell about a strained or fractured relationship with a family member, friend or colleague at work.

PERSONAL REFLECTION. How has resentment or anger from a broken relationship affected you?

Read Genesis 30:25—31:55.

1. Why does Jacob want to leave, and why does Laban want him to stay (30:25-30)?

2. What arrangement does Jacob suggest for wages (30:31-33)?

3. What is Laban's strategy in 30:34-38?

4. Describe Jacob's way of getting back at Laban to increase the strength of his own flocks (30:37-43).

5. How do you think these two men could have reacted in a better way to prevent their growing conflict?

6. What new factors in Jacob's situation now prompt him to quit working for Laban and return home (31:1-13)?

7. How does Rachel and Leah's reply confirm his decision (31:14-21)?

8. Looking at 31:11-21, how do you see that God has protected and provided for Jacob in the midst of his unjust treatment by Laban?

9. How can Jacob's experience give us hope when we are unfairly treated by our friends, spouse or employer?

10. How do Laban and Jacob defend their actions (31:22-42)?

11. Why is it so difficult for us to see the other's point of view in a disagreement?

12. How do Jacob and Laban reconcile their differences, and how does their effort strike you (31:43-55)?

13. What have you seen in this passage that can help you deal with a strained or fractured relationship?

Thank God that even in the midst of unfair treatment he does not desert his children.

Now or Later

Decide now what steps you can take toward a person with whom you are in conflict, and pray for courage to follow through.

18

Jacob Meets Esau: Planning, Prayer & Struggle

Genesis 32—33

The Christian life is a mysterious mixture of God's work and ours, his gracious provision and our effort. Sometimes we are perplexed over who should make the next move.

GROUP DISCUSSION. In what situation have you felt called to combine prayer and planning for an important activity?

PERSONAL REFLECTION. How has God revealed his will to you through a special set of events?

Jacob felt the tension of how to follow God's will as he returned to his father's house after a twenty-year absence. *Read Genesis 32:1-21.*

1. What effect would meeting the angels of God have on Jacob as he nears his encounter with Esau (32:1-2)?

2. How would you describe the tone of Jacob's message to Esau (32:3-5)?

_____

3. How does Jacob react to the report in verses 6-8?

_____

4. How does Jacob's prayer reflect his relationship with God (32:9-12)?

_____

5. In what ways can Jacob's prayer be a model for our own praying?

_____

6. To what extent do you think Jacob's plans are consistent with his prayer?

_____

7. *Read Genesis 32:22-32.* How does this struggle with the unknown man give insight to Jacob's personality?

_____

8. In what ways does Jacob emerge both stronger and weaker?

9. How does the change of name from *Jacob* to *Israel* indicate the development of his character?

10. What speaks to you from Jacob's experience about your own struggle to trust and obey the Lord?

11. *Read Genesis 33.* How does this meeting between Jacob and Esau contrast with the last time they saw each other (33:1-4)?

12. When Jacob settles in Shechem (33:18) he builds an altar. How do you think his encounter with Esau helped him understand the faithfulness of God (33:12-20)?

13. In what ways can Jacob's actions toward Esau be a model for us of repentance and reconciliation?

Ask God to show you how Jacob's story can help you face a difficult relationship in your own life.

Now or Later

Reflect on an experience in your own life that helps you appreciate God's faithfulness.

19

Jacob's Compromise & Commitment: The Cost of Discipleship

Genesis 34—36

In our Christian life both compromise and commitment can be costly. When we falter, the consequences take their toll on us personally and often on our family and friends. Nevertheless, God graciously calls us to repentance and renewed commitment.

GROUP DISCUSSION. Share a situation in which your compromise of a principle produced unfortunate results for others as well as yourself.

PERSONAL REFLECTION. Trace a way that God has enabled you to cope with the consequences of a compromise and continue on the right path.

Read Genesis 34.

---

1. What is Shechem's attitude toward Dinah, and how does his father try to compensate for the wrong done to her (34:1-12)?

2. How do you respond to the reaction of Jacob's sons and the measures they take for revenge (34:8-29)?

3. What does Jacob's response to this tragedy show about the public consequences of a private action?

4. *Read Genesis 35:1-15.* What were God's instructions to Jacob, and what was the cost of carrying them out (35:1-7)?

5. What "foreign god" in your life might be taking the place of God?

6. What specific step of obedience do you need to take along the path of discipleship?

7. What specific promises does God affirm to Jacob and his descendants (35:8-15)?

8. *Read Genesis 35:16-29.* Describe the new griefs that now come into Jacob's life.

9. What does changing his child's name from "son of my trouble" to Benjamin, "son of my right hand," tell us about Jacob's attitude toward his youngest son?

---

10. How can we, like Jacob, transform the pain of losing someone we love into courage for the future?

---

11. What final picture do we have of Isaac and his sons in 35:27-29?

---

12. What is the most significant lesson you have learned from the lives of these two brothers, Jacob and Esau?

Thank God that he is with us in our days of distress, even as he was with Jacob.

Now or Later

Looking back over the life of Jacob, trace the ways in which the consequences of his actions and God's gracious intervention shaped his character to make him a man of faith.

20

Joseph & His Brothers: Pride & Prejudice

Genesis 37—38

We often see how children tend to duplicate the weaknesses as well as the strengths of their parents. This trait is as evident in Old Testament families as it is today.

GROUP DISCUSSION. What strengths and weaknesses have you experienced in your own family?

PERSONAL REFLECTION. How have the strengths and weaknesses of your family affected you?

Jacob suffered as a boy from parental favoritism. Now we see how he perpetuates this practice in his relationship with Joseph—with disastrous results. *Read Genesis 37.*

1. How would you describe family relationships at the outset of the story (37:1-4)?

2. What kind of boy does Joseph appear to be?

3. In 37:5-11 how are the symbols in Joseph's two dreams interpreted by his family?

4. What are the varied reactions of Joseph's brothers when they see him coming (37:12-22)?

5. How do you think Joseph feels as he overhears their conversation (37:23-27)?

6. What plan does Judah propose, and why does it appeal to his brothers (37:25-28)?

7. What various motives do you see in the way the brothers report the news of Joseph's disappearance to their father (37:29-35)?

8. To what extent are you involved in a family situation with some of these elements, and what can you do to relieve the tension?

9. *Read Genesis 38.* When Judah finds his lineage in jeopardy in spite of having three sons, what does he do about it (38:1-11)?

10. What strategy does Tamar work out to establish her status as matriarch of Judah's line (38:12-30)?

11. In what ways today do you see God working his purposes for good in spite of evil and tragedy?

12. How can these chapters encourage us to trust God in the midst of difficult circumstances?

Thank God for his long view in working out his plans in spite of our sins and failures.

Now or Later

Look at the parallels in the deception of Isaac by Jacob and of Jacob by his sons, and the results.

21

Slave & Prisoner: Performance Under Pressure

Genesis 39—40

How do you react when you are treated unjustly? How do you feel when you do everything you can to serve God well, only to have the bottom drop out of your life?

GROUP DISCUSSION. Share a time in your life when you felt you were treated unfairly.

PERSONAL REFLECTION. What is your attitude toward people who believe unjust accusations about you?

Joseph faced unfair treatment after he became a slave in Egypt. His example of perseverance under pressure and the way he coped with a shattering reverse can be helpful to us in similar difficulties. *Read Genesis 39.*

---

1. What are the steps to Joseph's success when he comes to Potiphar's house (39:1-6)?

2. Describe the increasing pressure Joseph now experiences (39:6-12).

---

3. What can we learn from the way he resists temptation?

---

4. How does Potiphar's wife put pressure on her husband to get revenge on Joseph (39:13-20)?

---

5. How do you suppose Joseph might feel about this second injustice?

---

6. When you have been in a situation where you were treated unjustly, how did you feel about God's letting it happen?

---

7. In what way does Joseph now seem different than when we saw him in his father's house?

---

8. As the chapter ends (39:20-23), how does Joseph's prison situation parallel his experience in Potiphar's house?

9. *Read Genesis 40.* Describe the new situation in which Joseph now finds himself (40:1-8).

---

10. In 40:9-19 how do the dreams and Joseph's interpretations differ?

---

11. What are the results for the cupbearer, the baker and Joseph (40:20-23)?

---

12. At this point how do you think Joseph feels?

---

13. What impresses you about Joseph in light of these incredible disappointments?

How can Joseph's example encourage us?

Thank God for giving us the example of Joseph's life.

Now or Later

Think about unfair treatment you have had in your life and how Joseph's example of grace under pressure speaks to you.

22

Joseph Governs Egypt: Faithful Service Rewarded

Genesis 41—42

We often take a short-term view of the Christian life that concentrates on what God does *for* us *now*. Yet God has long-range purposes that focus on what he wants to accomplish *in* us for the *future*.

GROUP DISCUSSION. In your life who has been a model of faithful service to God without visible reward?

PERSONAL REFLECTION. Think of someone whose example has encouraged you in your service for God. Thank God for that person.

Through adversity and disappointment God has been developing Joseph's character and has given him invaluable training. Now a sudden crisis reveals what kind of person he has become. *Read Genesis 41.*

1. What were Pharaoh's dreams, and why did they trouble him (41:1-8)?

2. How is Joseph brought into the situation (41:9-16)?

What impresses you about Joseph as he comes from prison to palace?

---

3. What do Joseph's interpretation of the dreams and his proposal demonstrate (41:17-36)?

---

4. Describe the responsibilities Pharaoh gives Joseph in 41:37-49.

---

5. In what ways had God prepared Joseph during these twelve years in Egypt?

---

6. How can Joseph's experience help you hang on during a time of hardship when there is little reward or appreciation?

---

7. What do you think the names of Joseph's two sons tell us about the contrast between his present situation and his arrival in Egypt?

---

8. *Read Genesis 42.* Trace the events which lead Joseph's brothers into his presence and fulfill his earlier dreams (42:1-11).

9. Why do you think Joseph accuses his brothers of being spies (42:12-20)?

10. Describe how the brothers react to Joseph's orders (42:21-24).

11. As they return home, how does their situation take a turn for the worse (42:25-38)?

12. In what ways does Reuben's response to his father's despair show his willingness to shoulder family responsibility (42:37)?

13. In what way has adversity or disappointment helped you become more mature in your responsibility to others?

Thank God that he is always watching over us.

Now or Later

Trace in your own life how you have seen God use a difficult assignment to prepare you for a later responsibility.

23

Family Reconciliation: Repentance & Responsibility

Genesis 43:1—45:15

What makes reconciliation possible? What elements are necessary on each side of a hurt or wrong in order to heal a damaged relationship? This study suggests answers for these crucial questions.

GROUP DISCUSSION. In our world where do you see the greatest need for reconciliation?

PERSONAL REFLECTION. In your life where do you feel need for reconciliation?

Joseph's brothers have now returned home from Egypt with a report of their traumatic experience. As the grain purchased on the first visit to Egypt runs out, Jacob and his sons face increasingly difficult decisions. Although our experience may be less traumatic, we can learn principles of reconciliation from this complex family situation. *Read Genesis 43.*

---

1. As the famine intensifies, what pressures does it put on Jacob and his sons (43:1-10)?

2. What impresses you about Jacob as he sends his sons off (43:11-14)?

3. Think of a difficult situation you are currently facing. How can you trust it to God Almighty, the one for whom nothing is impossible?

4. In 43:15-25 how do the brothers interpret Joseph's intentions?

5. What insights into Joseph's character to you see in 43:26-34?

6. *Read Genesis 44.* What final strategy does Joseph devise, and how does it test the brothers' character and loyalty (44:1-17)?

7. What does Judah's attitude in 44:18-34 show about the changes that have taken place in him and his brothers since their betrayal of Joseph twenty-three years earlier?

8. Restoring a relationship fractured by injustice and injury requires repentance, confession and acceptance of responsibility for the consequences. In what way have you, like Joseph's brothers, been involved in such a process?

---

9. *Read Genesis 45:1-15.* How does Joseph explain to his brothers the reason for his being sold into Egypt and the purpose of his sufferings?

---

10. How can this perspective toward your own suffering make it possible for you to forgive someone who has grievously hurt you?

---

11. To what extent can Joseph's experience give us greater confidence in God's sovereignty over the events of our lives?

Ask God to give you the will to forgive one person in your life who has hurt you.

Now or Later

What other attitudes and actions might Joseph have shown to his brothers? Reflect on his *choice* to forgive and see God's hand at work in the circumstances of his life.

24

Jacob in Egypt: God Preserves His People

Genesis 45:16—47:31

Do you ever wonder how the bits and pieces of your life fit together? Seeing God at work in the Bible can strengthen our faith and hope as we work through difficult situations we cannot understand.

GROUP DISCUSSION. What prayer request are you patiently waiting for God to fulfill?

PERSONAL REFLECTION. Reflect on some promise that sustains you as you wait for God to work in a specific way.

This study shows how the seemingly unrelated and perplexing events of the preceding chapters now serve God's purpose during the famine. *Read Genesis 45:16—46:27.*

1. What is Pharaoh's reaction to the news that Joseph's brothers have arrived (45:16-24)?

2. What would this mean to the brothers, with their burden of guilt and fear?

3. Describe Jacob's reaction to the astounding news his sons bring back from Egypt (45:25-28).

4. How does God encourage Jacob in the present and for the future (46:1-4)?

5. When has God allowed you to see how seemingly unrelated events fit into the tapestry of his will for you?

6. How does 46:5-27 underscore God's faithfulness to the promises he made to Abraham, Isaac and Jacob?

7. *Read Genesis 46:28—47:12.* In what ways does Joseph's skill as a planner and administrator continue to be demonstrated as he arranges for his father's family (46:28-34)?

8. Describe the encounter of Joseph's brothers with Pharaoh (47:1-6).

9. What impresses you about Jacob, so recently in despair and ready to die, in his interview with Pharaoh (47:7-10)?

10. *Read Genesis 47:13-31.* How does Joseph's continuing strategy save the lives of the Egyptians (47:13-26)?

11. In what ways does Jacob's last request of Joseph show his faith in God's promise regarding his descendants and their own land (47:27-31)?

12. How can Joseph's story help you trust God in perplexing areas of your life?

Thank God that he is faithful and always keeps his promises.

Now or Later

What is your attitude right now regarding your particular circumstances? Spend time praying or journaling about this.

25

Jacob's Blessing: The Life of Faith

Genesis 48—49

Our self-centered technological society seeks instant gratification and immediate results. The "good life" emblazoned on television is measured by what we have and use *now*. The elderly are usually considered obsolete rather than examples of how to live fully for the long run. Yet they are a resource, teaching us valuable lessons about persevering in the life of faith.

GROUP DISCUSSION. What older person has had an impact on your life and why?

PERSONAL REFLECTION. How do you picture yourself in old age?

This study views Jacob's final days as he evaluates the past and looks into the future. *Read Genesis 48.*

1. How will Jacob's adoption of Joseph's sons Ephraim and Manasseh affect their share in the promises God made to Jacob (48:1-7)?

2. In what ways is Jacob's faith evident as he blesses Ephraim and Manasseh (48:8-22)?

3. How does Jacob sum up the way God has dealt with him over the years?

4. Describe God in terms of the way he has been working in your life.

5. *Read Genesis 49.* In 49:1-7 how are the blessings given to Reuben, Simeon and Levi related to their past actions (see Genesis 34; 35:22)?

6. Although our past failures and sins affect our future, how can God's forgiveness and grace help us triumph over these consequences?

7. What future does Jacob see for Judah in 49:8-12?

8. What characteristics of the Messiah's reign does Jacob foretell?

9. After Jacob blesses six of his other sons in 49:13-21, how does the blessing he gives to Joseph show awareness of all Joseph has been through (49:22-28)?

10. As you look at the names given to God in 49:24-25, which have special meaning for you?

11. How do Jacob's last words demonstrate the faith and hope with which he finishes the course of his life (49:29-33)?

12. Looking back over Jacob's life, what element provides an encouragement or challenge for you?

In the words of an old hymn, "Praise him for all that is past, and trust him for all that's to come."

Now or Later

Recall the events in Joseph's life which illustrate the names of God in Genesis 49:24-25.

26

Joseph's Final Years: Forgiveness, Love & Hope

Genesis 50

Like a fine painting or sculpture, God's work takes time. But its result is a tribute to the artist. When you look back at even your recent past, you may be able to see God's work beginning to take shape.

GROUP DISCUSSION. Think of someone who has injured you. What is your attitude toward that person?

PERSONAL REFLECTION. What barriers in your life have kept you from forgiveness and reconciliation?

The previous studies have shown how God used years of hardship and suffering to produce in Joseph a spiritual maturity unsurpassed in the Old Testament. In this final chapter of Genesis we see how his life reflects the character of God. Joseph provides a model for the way we should relate to God and others. *Read Genesis 50.*

---

1. How are Joseph's love and respect for his father evident (vv. 1-14)?

2. What light does this ceremony throw on Joseph's authority and prestige in Egypt?

3. Describe the reaction of the brothers after their father's burial, and the strategy they devise to protect themselves (vv. 15-18).

4. Why do you think Joseph reacts as he does (v. 17)?

5. What is his explanation of what has happened to him (vv. 19-20)?

6. How can Joseph's example help you deal with unfair treatment in your own life?

7. How does Joseph show his brothers that he not only forgives but genuinely loves them (v. 21)?

8. If you have been wronged by someone, what action may God want you to take—beyond the usual "forgive and forget" attitude—to demonstrate a loving concern for that person's welfare?

9. How are Joseph's final years and words in verses 22-26 similar to his father's?

10. As you look back over this chapter, how do you see Joseph demonstrating the qualities of forgiveness, love and hope?

11. How has your vision of God been enlarged through your study of Genesis?

12. What has God shown you through this study that will stay with you?

Take time to thank God for his goodness, grace and faithfulness in each generation, including your own.

Now or Later

In the Genesis narrative we have seen that Abraham, Isaac and Jacob died in faith, looking forward to promises they did not see fulfilled in their lifetime. How does their example provide a model for our hope as Christians?

Leader's Notes

Leading a Bible discussion can be an enjoyable and rewarding experience. But it can also be *scary*—especially if you've never done it before. If this is your feeling, you're in good company. When God asked Moses to lead the Israelites out of Egypt, he replied, "O Lord, please send someone else to do it"! (Ex 4:13). It was the same with Solomon, Jeremiah and Timothy, but God helped these people in spite of their weaknesses, and he will help you as well.

You don't need to be an expert on the Bible or a trained teacher to lead a Bible discussion. The idea behind these inductive studies is that the leader guides group members to discover for themselves what the Bible has to say. This method of learning will allow group members to remember much more of what is said than a lecture would.

These studies are designed to be led easily. As a matter of fact, the flow of questions through the passage from observation to interpretation to application is so natural that you may feel that the studies lead themselves. This study guide is also flexible. You can use it with a variety of groups—student, professional, neighborhood or church groups. Each study takes forty-five to sixty minutes in a group setting.

There are some important facts to know about group dynamics and encouraging discussion. The suggestions listed below should enable you to effectively and enjoyably fulfill your role as leader.

Preparing for the Study

1. Ask God to help you understand and apply the passage in your own life. Unless this happens, you will not be prepared to lead others. Pray too for the various members of the group. Ask God to open your hearts to the message of his Word and motivate you to action.

2. Read the introduction to the entire guide to get an overview of the entire book and the issues which will be explored.

3. As you begin each study, read and reread the assigned Bible passage to

familiarize yourself with it.

4. This study guide is based on the New International Version of the Bible. It will help you and the group if you use this translation as the basis for your study and discussion.

5. Carefully work through each question in the study. Spend time in meditation and reflection as you consider how to respond.

6. Write your thoughts and responses in the space provided in the study guide. This will help you to express your understanding of the passage clearly.

7. It might help to have a Bible dictionary handy. Use it to look up any unfamiliar words, names or places. (For additional help on how to study a passage, see chapter five of *How to Lead a LifeBuilder Study*, IVP, 2018.)

8. Consider how you can apply the Scripture to your life. Remember that the group will follow your lead in responding to the studies. They will not go any deeper than you do.

9. Once you have finished your own study of the passage, familiarize yourself with the leader's notes for the study you are leading. These are designed to help you in several ways. First, they tell you the purpose the study guide author had in mind when writing the study. Take time to think through how the study questions work together to accomplish that purpose. Second, the notes provide you with additional background information or suggestions on group dynamics for various questions. This information can be useful when people have difficulty understanding or answering a question. Third, the leader's notes can alert you to potential problems you may encounter during the study.

10. If you wish to remind yourself of anything mentioned in the leader's notes, make a note to yourself below that question in the study.

Leading the Study

1. Begin the study on time. Open with prayer, asking God to help the group to understand and apply the passage.

2. Be sure that everyone in your group has a study guide. Encourage the group to prepare beforehand for each discussion by reading the introduction to the guide and by working through the questions in the study.

3. At the beginning of your first time together, explain that these studies are meant to be discussions, not lectures. Encourage the members of the group to participate. However, do not put pressure on those who may be hesitant to speak during the first few sessions. You may want to suggest the following guidelines to your group.

☐ Stick to the topic being discussed.

☐ Your responses should be based on the verses which are the focus of the discussion and not on outside authorities such as commentaries or speakers.

☐ These studies focus on a particular passage of Scripture. Only rarely should you refer to other portions of the Bible. This allows for everyone to participate in in-depth study on equal ground.

☐ Anything said in the group is considered confidential and will not be discussed outside the group unless specific permission is given to do so.

☐ We will listen attentively to each other and provide time for each person present to talk.

☐ We will pray for each other.

4. Have a group member read the introduction at the beginning of the discussion.

5. Every session begins with a group discussion question. The question or activity is meant to be used before the passage is read. The question introduces the theme of the study and encourages group members to begin to open up. Encourage as many members as possible to participate, and be ready to get the discussion going with your own response.

This section is designed to reveal where our thoughts or feelings need to be transformed by Scripture. That is why it is especially important not to read the passage before the discussion question is asked. The passage will tend to color the honest reactions people would otherwise give because they are, of course, supposed to think the way the Bible does.

You may want to supplement the group discussion question with an icebreaker to help people to get comfortable. See the community section of the *Small Group Starter Kit* (IVP, 1995) for more ideas.

You also might want to use the personal reflection question with your group. Either allow a time of silence for people to respond individually or discuss it together.

6. Have a group member (or members if the passage is long) read aloud the passage to be studied. Then give people several minutes to read the passage again silently so that they can take it all in.

7. Question 1 will generally be an overview question designed to briefly survey the passage. Encourage the group to look at the whole passage, but try to avoid getting sidetracked by questions or issues that will be addressed later in the study.

8. As you ask the questions, keep in mind that they are designed to be used just as they are written. You may simply read them aloud. Or you may prefer to express them in your own words.

There may be times when it is appropriate to deviate from the study guide. For example, a question may have already been answered. If so, move on to the next question. Or someone may raise an important question not covered in the guide. Take time to discuss it, but try to keep the group from going off on tangents.

9. Avoid answering your own questions. If necessary, repeat or

rephrase them until they are clearly understood. Or point out something you read in the leader's notes to clarify the context or meaning. An eager group quickly becomes passive and silent if they think the leader will do most of the talking.

10. Don't be afraid of silence. People may need time to think about the question before formulating their answers.

11. Don't be content with just one answer. Ask, "What do the rest of you think?" or "Anything else?" until several people have given answers to the question.

12. Acknowledge all contributions. Try to be affirming whenever possible. Never reject an answer. If it is clearly off-base, ask, "Which verse led you to that conclusion?" or again, "What do the rest of you think?"

13. Don't expect every answer to be addressed to you, even though this will probably happen at first. As group members become more at ease, they will begin to truly interact with each other. This is one sign of healthy discussion.

14. Don't be afraid of controversy. It can be very stimulating. If you don't resolve an issue completely, don't be frustrated. Move on and keep it in mind for later. A subsequent study may solve the problem.

15. Periodically summarize what the group has said about the passage. This helps to draw together the various ideas mentioned and gives continuity to the study. But don't preach.

16. At the end of the Bible discussion you may want to allow group members a time of quiet to work on an idea under "Now or Later." Then discuss what you experienced. Or you may want to encourage group members to work on these ideas between meetings. Give an opportunity during the session for people to talk about what they are learning.

17. Conclude your time together with conversational prayer, adapting the prayer suggestion at the end of the study to your group. Ask for God's help in following through on the commitments you've made.

18. End on time.

Many more suggestions and helps are found in *How to Lead a LifeBuilder Study.*

Components of Small Groups

A healthy small group should do more than study the Bible. There are four components to consider as you structure your time together.

Nurture. Small groups help us to grow in our knowledge and love of God. Bible study is the key to making this happen and is the foundation of your small group.

Community. Small groups are a great place to develop deep friendships with other Christians. Allow time for informal interaction before and after each study. Plan activities and games that will help you get to know each other. Spend time having fun together—going on a picnic or cooking dinner together.

Worship and prayer. Your study will be enhanced by spending time praising God together in prayer or song. Pray for each other's needs—and keep track of how God is answering prayer in your group. Ask God to help you to apply what you are learning in your study.

Outreach. Reaching out to others can be a practical way of applying what you are learning, and it will keep your group from becoming self-focused. Host a series of evangelistic discussions for your friends or neighbors. Clean up the yard of an elderly friend. Serve at a soup kitchen together, or spend a day working in the community.

Many more suggestions and helps in each of these areas are found in the *Small Group Starter Kit.* You will also find information on building a small group. Reading through the starter kit will be worth your time.

Part 1: Creation & Primeval History
Study 1. Genesis 1:1—2:3.
The Creation.
Purpose: To consider the greatness of the Creator and the magnificence of his creation as well as our special place in the world.

General note. Inductive Bible study calls for faithfulness to the inspired text. The discussion needs to be informed and guided by the passage. As we open our minds and hearts to its message, the Holy Spirit will illuminate the Scripture and apply it to our individual needs.

Resist the temptation to share what you have learned from the notes. Taking on the role of a teacher keeps the members from their own discovery. Your challenge as a leader is to keep the discussion from getting into unrelated topics, no matter how interesting they may appear. Remember that the goal is not to master the biblical passage, but to help the members hear for themselves a relevant word from the Lord.

Group discussion. This item is designed to help the members get acquainted. Keep your eye on the clock to prevent this discussion from taking time that should be spent on the Bible study.

Question 1. Have three volunteers read Genesis 1:1-13, 14-25 and 1:26—2:3. Although everything has a beginning, God has always existed.

Question 3. Someone may ask about the length of the days. Over the centuries the meaning of the word *day* has been vigorously debated. There have been four main interpretations: (1) each day represents a twenty-four hour period; (2) the days are long periods that can be correlated with geological epochs; (3) the writer saw creation in a series of six visions given over six days; and (4) the days are arranged in a literary structure that does not intend to give chronological sequence or duration.

"The earth was formless and empty" (Genesis 1:2)					
Creative Commands	Day No.	Elements	Creative Commands	Day No.	Elements
1. verse 3	1	Light	5. verse 14	4	Lights & Stars
2. verse 6	2	Air & Water	6. verse 20	5	Birds & Fish
3. verse 9	3	Land	7. verse 24	6	Animals
4. verse 11		Vegetation	8. verse 26		Humankind

These two sets are parallel, first *forming* and then *filling* the world.

Do not let the group bog down in discussion of these views. The meaning of *day* cannot be decided on the basis of this chapter alone, nor is it necessary to decide which view is correct in order to appreciate the author's message. Remember, this account was first given to Israel when they were coming out of slavery in Egypt and needed to know the *Who* of creation, not the *how*. Genesis 1 does not comment on the method of creation; it focuses on the power of God's creative word and the magnificence of the results.

Question 6. Encourage the group to think concretely rather than abstractly. Each of us has chaotic, ugly or discordant areas in our lives. Some of these should be specifically identified during the discussion. You can make them items of prayer at the end of your study.

Question 7. Note that ancient kings often *wore* the image of their god. Genesis affirms that every person is *made* in the image of God. That involves—at the very least—awareness of self, ability to make choices, sense of community and creativity.

Question 8. "Rule over" does not mean exploitation. Humankind was to rule over the animal world even as God does—for their own good.

God provides food. In ancient myths and religions the gods created humanity as an afterthought. In Genesis we see creating Adam and Eve as God's goal in creation; their welfare was God's supreme concern.

Study 2. Genesis 2:4-25. Adam & Eve.

Purpose: To understand who we were meant to be in relation to God, nature and each other.

Question 1. Have volunteers read Genesis 2:4-25, one paragraph at a time.

Question 2. The Hebrew word for "man" (*adam*) sounds like the word for "ground" (*adamah*). Humanity doesn't "have" a body and a spirit, as frequently thought, but rather becomes "a living being," a unity.

Question 3. The Hebrew word *eden* means "delight." This geographical description indicates that Eden was not an allegorical or mythical setting but an actual location.

Question 4. Since the nature of the tree of the knowledge of good and evil is not explained, do not spend time speculating on its meaning. Rather point out that in the context the main point is the *prohibition* and not the *properties* of this tree.

Question 7. For the Hebrews a name usually had a special meaning. It often described the character or significance of a person or place. Adam's naming of these creatures would show insight into their nature.

In this chapter the writer uses two names for God: *Yahweh* (which is translated "LORD") is his personal name, and *Elohim* (which is translated "God") is his title.

Question 8. The term *suitable helper* literally means "a help as opposite him," in other words, "corresponding to him." The connotation is more *cooperation with* than *service to* another.

Matthew Henry comments on God's choice of a rib to create Eve:

> Not made out of his head to top him,
> not out of his feet to be trampled upon,
> but out of his side to be equal with him,
>   under his arm to be protected and
>   near to his heart to be loved.

Study 3. Genesis 3. The First Sin.

Purpose: To see how sin initially entered the world, and to learn something about the way we can be tempted to disobey God.

Question 1. Have the members volunteer for the roles of narrator, God, Adam, Eve and the serpent, then read the chapter aloud like a drama.

Notice how devious and concerted the serpent's strategy is. He begins by asking questions intended to obscure God's command (v. 1). Next, he flatly contradicts God's warning about eating from the tree (v. 4). Then he misrepresents God's motive (v. 5). This strategy encourages Eve to make her own decision about the value of obeying God.

Question 6. Adam and Eve's response to their nakedness has nothing to do with sexual guilt or shame. The Bible has a high view of sex, despite certain church teachings throughout the centuries. Just as their nakedness was a sign of innocence and lack of self-consciousness, it now becomes a symbol of guilt to be covered up so they can still appear presentable.

Question 8. Adam and Eve made many mistakes. They listened to the creature instead of the Creator, followed their own way instead of God's instruction, doubted God's concern for their best interest and made self-fulfillment their goal.

Question 10. The result of their sin was profound disorder. They experienced relational estrangement with one another and with God, and they were put into battle with evil.

Question 11. God knows good and evil habitually by choosing the good and rejecting the evil. We know good and evil by the guilty experience of an evil choice. God's action in sending Adam and Eve out of the garden is also a protection. He does not want them to eat out of the tree of eternal life in their present broken state (vv. 22-23).

Question 12. The experience of temptation itself is not a sin. Martin Luther once said that while we may not be able to stop the birds from flying overhead, we can keep them from building nests in our hair.

Study 4. Genesis 4—5. Cain & Abel.

Purpose: To gain insight into the way wrong attitudes lead to sinful actions. Also to see how God desires to help us resist temptation and overcome evil.

Question 1. Have volunteers for the roles of narrator, Eve, God, Cain and Lamech read aloud chapter 4.

Question 2. Note that the author doesn't tell us the exact nature of Cain's offering. The text says Cain brought *some* fruits as an offering, but Abel brought *fat* portions from the firstborn. Abel's offering might not have been inherently superior to Cain's, but his attitude in the giving might have been.

Throughout these studies the group should avoid reading into the text unwarranted questions and explanations. The main ideas in the biblical passage can usually be grasped from careful study of the author's words and their context.

Question 7. The names in this chapter continue to be significant. *Cain* means "brought forth" or "acquired" (v. 1). *Nod* means "wandering."

Question 9. Biblical genealogies are provided to trace descendants and not to calculate a span of time. Sometimes generations are omitted. For example, Matthew's stylized scheme has three sets of fourteen generations (Mt 1:1-17) and leaves out three successive kings. So the names in Genesis should be understood as separate landmarks rather than continuous links. Biblical genealogies also serve to bear witness to the historical nature of the record. Furthermore, the Genesis narratives often present the patriarchs not simply as individuals with small families but as heads of clans. Tribal relationships are expressed as families in the hereditary line. In Genesis genealogies sometimes refer to a clan rather than an individual (for example, see Gen 10:4).

Question 12. If time permits, scan chapter 5 to trace the line from Seth to Noah—the subject of the next study.

Study 5. Genesis 6—7. The Flood.

Purpose: To consider how Noah's example can be an encouragement to us amid our struggles in an evil world.

Question 1. These "sons of God" (v. 2) may be sons of Seth, angels or royal sons named after gods. Although we aren't sure exactly who they are, apparently their activity is wrong and represents the spread of sin in another

dimension. The Nephilim are probably giants (see Num 13:33). Focus atten-
tion on the rest of the passage, where the meaning is all too clear.

Question 3. Basil Atkinson comments on the cost of creating humanity with
freedom of choice. "Here we see God's vulnerability. Here is the pain of creative love. Here is the wounded spirit of the artist whose work is rejected, the
broken heart of the lover whose love is not returned. God himself enters the
world of brokenness and pain. Genesis six reveals the Suffering God. 'The
tears of God are the meaning of history'" (*The Message of Genesis 1—11*
[Downers Grove, Ill.: InterVarsity Press, 1990], p. 137).

Question 7. A covenant is different from a contract in one major respect: a
contract is valid only when both parties continue to observe its requirements.
God's covenant, however, remains operative even when his people fail to
honor their part of the agreement.

Question 8. The story of God's protective love is also the story of Noah's
faithful obedience. There can be an intimacy with God out in the field with
hammer and saw just as much as at the altar.

Question 11. "The Lord decrees that the waters of judgment will wipe out
humankind from the earth. Yet he shuts up Noah and his family in the ark.
The water which is the means of judgment for the world is at the same time
the means of salvation for Noah's family. In this one action there is judgment
and mercy" (Ibid., p. 138).

Question 12. From the narrative itself we cannot determine whether the
flood was local or universal. The biblical use of *all* and *every* is relative to the
situation and context. For example, in Colossians 1:23 Paul states that the
gospel has been preached "to every creature under heaven," obviously meaning the known world. Likewise, the Hebrew word for "earth" (*erets*) is frequently translated "land" and "country." Whether earth should be
understood locally or universally in chapters 6—7 must be determined by the
broader context of Genesis and the author's historical perspective.

Study 6. Genesis 8:1—9:17. The Rainbow.

Purpose: To consider the example of Noah and the gracious fulfillment of
God's promises.

Question 1. Consider both those in the ark and God's activity to end the
flood (8:1-5). In the Old Testament, God's "remembering" is more than men-
tal recall. It always emphasizes his movement toward what he remembers in
faithful love and timely intervention.

Question 2. Olive trees don't grow at high levels but in the lowlands. This
event shows how much the earth has dried up.

Question 5. Note that seven of each clean animal and bird have been pre-
served (7:2) to provide for this sacrifice without destroying its kind.

Question 7. "Smells the pleasing aroma" is a figurative way of saying that

God delights in his children's worship. Jürgen Moltmann writes, "The promise never again to destroy all flesh because of its wickedness is an unconditional promise on God's part. It is God's indestructible Yes to his creation . . . Not even human wickedness can thwart the Creator's will toward his creation . . . God remains true to the earth for God remains true to himself."

Question 9. In the Bible, blood represents life. Here God makes it clear that the life of his creatures, and especially human life, ultimately belongs to him.

Question 11. Derek Kidner writes, "The sign of the rainbow is well-suited to fulfill the prime function of all covenant signs which is reassurance . . . The obvious glory of the rainbow against the gloom of the cloud seems enough to make it a token of grace. . . . The promise is not that a rainbow will be seen in every cloud, but when it is seen God will remember his covenant" (*Genesis* [Downers Grove, Ill.: InterVarsity Press, 1978], p. 102).

Study 7. Genesis 9:18—11:32. The Tower of Babel.

Purpose: To see how sin spreads from generation to generation in both family and community, resulting in God's judgment and gracious intervention.

General note. This long passage has three main sections: Noah's drunkenness (9:18-28), genealogies (10:1-32), and tower of Babel and more genealogies (11:1-32)

Question 1. The word *earth* in verse 19 can also mean "land" or "country," that is, the Near East families and nations with whom the Pentateuch is primarily concerned.

It's hard for us to understand the gravity of Ham's sin. The Old Testament and other ancient cultures took a son's respectful duty to his father very seriously. The human father represented God. To curse or strike a father (or mother) was punishable by death.

Question 5. Although this genealogy focuses on the special line from Noah through Shem which leads to Abraham, it continues to comment on other families and emphasizes the unity of the human race. Don't spend much time on this question.

Question 6. Shinar (11:1) is Babylonia, a city which came increasingly to symbolize a godless society whose sins reach to heaven. This event at Babel involves Ham's descendants in the line of Cush and Nimrod (10:8-10).

Question 9. Ten generations are noted, perhaps to match the ten named from Adam to Noah. The growth of nations in chapter 10 makes it clear that great intervals lie between names. The life span steadily declines toward the 175 years of Abraham.

Questions 10-11. These questions provide a wrap-up to all of section one. This is also a good time to talk more broadly about how things are going for your group. In particular you might discuss how members are doing with the inductive method of study. For example, to what extent is the discussion directly related to the passage being studied? How much of the members' knowledge about Genesis is coming from what they are discovering for themselves in the book?

Part 2: Abraham, Isaac & Jacob—The Emergence of Israel
Study 8. Genesis 12—13. Abram's Call.
Purpose: To see that faith requires Abram and us to trust God with the unknown.
Question 1. Abram grew up in the highly civilized city of Ur on the Euphrates River in southern Babylonia. Archaeologists have discovered that it had running water, two-story houses and a banking system. So Abram was being asked to leave a very comfortable existence. For the rest of his life he would live in tents.

Both Ur and Haran were centers of moon worship, which may be the reason the migration halted where it did. While Abram had already heard God's call (Acts 7:2-4), Terah's motive for leaving may have been for safety. Since the Elamites destroyed Ur around 1950 B.C., this move might well have saved their lives.
Question 3. Shechem lies in a pass between two mountains at the crossroads of central Palestine. It would prove to be a place of decision for Israel at crucial times during the following centuries.
Question 10. As the older man, Abram would have the right to choose the best land.
Question 11. Abram built an altar to the Lord who had promised him the land. In this way he claimed the area as the Lord's gift to his descendants. For considerable periods Abram lived there himself in a conscious possession of the right to the land.

Study 9. Genesis 14—15. Conflict & Covenant.
Purpose: To observe how God carefully nurtures and strengthens Abram's faith and ours.
Question 1. This narrative has a wealth of geographical detail. It traces the invasion route of the Eastern kings along the ancient international caravan road running north and south. Here for the first time biblical events are explicitly correlated with external history. This chronicle of a secular military operation suddenly assumes religious significance with the intervention of Abram, who occupies a central role in the second part of the narrative. This incident is the first example of God's fulfilling his promise that Abram's name would become great and blessed.
Question 3. Since Abram lived in tents away from the cities, his people were not involved in this military campaign.
Question 8. Have volunteers read the parts of narrator, the Lord and Abram in chapter 15.

In Abram's culture a childless man could adopt an heir to fulfill the responsibilities of a son.

Question 10. Abram believed the Lord. "He accepted God's reassurance. The verb form suggests an ongoing activity, i.e., he kept believing the promise, he kept relying on the Lord" (*The New Bible Commentary* [Downers Grove, Ill.: InterVarsity Press, 1994], p. 72).

Question 11. In this covenant ritual the two parties to an agreement passed between the two halves of the dead animals to invoke a similar fate on themselves if they should break their pledge. Abram sits on one side and waits for God to take the initiative to emphasize the fact that he alone makes the covenant. The wording here exactly follows the contemporary legal form for a treaty. First comes the identification and historical introduction (v. 7), then a statement of the future relationship and obligation (vv. 18-19). But unlike human treaties, this one is unilateral and unconditional, as God assumes an obligation without imposing reciprocal responsibilities on Abram.

Study 10. Genesis 16—17. Ishmael & Isaac.

Purpose: To help us realize that God has the power to fulfill his promises to us in spite of our circumstances.

Question 1. Have volunteers for the roles of narrator, Sarai, Abram, Hagar and the Lord read aloud this minidrama in chapter 16.

Question 2. Middle Eastern culture of the time sanctioned this way of obtaining children. Archaeologists have discovered Muzi marriage contracts with this stipulation inserted by the husband to guard against the possibility of being left without an heir.

Question 4. Hagar shows false pride, Sarai unjust blame and Abram unwarranted neutrality, although later he assumes his responsibility in naming Hagar's son *Ishmael.*

Question 5. God's nurturing care is extended to a slave, an outcast woman.

Question 9. In the ancient Near East a person's name was intertwined with the essence of his or her being and personality. In the Bible name-giving has great importance. A change of name is an event of major significance, symbolizing a new character and destiny. Each of the patriarchs—Abraham, Isaac and Jacob—received his name from God himself. These names, as well as those of the great biblical heroes like Moses and Aaron, David and Solomon, are unique, not given to any other person in the Bible.

Question 10. Circumcision was practiced by the Egyptians, among other nations, as a tribal rite of puberty. Here God adapts and transforms an existing custom by giving it a radically new meaning. For God's people circumcision is a divinely ordained sign of the covenant performed on the eighth day after birth, a physical act of identification and dedication as a member of the covenant community.

Question 12. Abraham laughs at the thought of himself and Sarah having a son at their age. But the Lord gets the last laugh. He names Abraham's son *Isaac,* which means "he laughs."

Study 11. Genesis 18—19. Sodom & Gomorrah.
Purpose: To show how one righteous man and his family are rescued by God, and to consider what we can do to avert the judgment of God on ourselves.
Question 1. Here we have the arrival of three men who appear to be ordinary travelers. But it soon becomes evident to Abraham that it is the Lord appearing to him in human form.
Question 4. Note the remarkable change in Abraham's perspective and attitude at this point. Until now his main concern, as God's chosen person to found a covenant nation, has been to separate himself from the pagan nations and to concentrate on producing a son. For example, Abraham's earlier involvement with Sodom (14:11-24) primarily concerned his own relatives, Lot and his family. Here he shows a broader interest in his concern for the fate of these two pagan cities, especially for any of their inhabitants who may be righteous. The narrative casts the father of the Jewish people in a representative role that foreshadows Israel's blessing to the whole world.

This conversation is not so much haggling or bargaining as it is exploring. Abraham is feeling his way forward in concern, faith and humility to learn more about God's rule, mercy and judgment in the world.
Question 7. The word *outcry* (18:20, 21; 19:13) also means "outrage." The Hebrew root indicates the anguished cry of the oppressed, the agonized plea of a victim of some great injustice.
Question 11. The natural ingredients of destruction were present in this region with its bitumen, petroleum, sulfur and salt. The destruction of these cities may well have been caused by one of the last earthquakes that shaped the lower Jordan Valley. Lightning could have ignited the gases to cause a terrible conflagration, raining down molten sulfur and salt and producing the smoke witnessed by Abraham (19:28). Whatever the natural causes, this occurrence was not a random disaster but a judgment effected by God for a specific purpose, at the prescribed time and with a moral significance.

In committing incest Lot's daughters put their desire for children above the moral law. Their offspring—the Moabites and the Ammonites—became two of Israel's major enemies throughout Israel's history.

Study 12. Genesis 20—21. Political & Family Crises.
Purpose: To encourage us to trust and obey God when we are tempted toward unbelief and disobedience.
Question 4. Abraham's answer shows that his fear and prejudgment of Abimelech's people (20:11) led to devious reasoning (20:12), shifting the

blame to God (20:13) and making the sacrifice of Sarah a test of her love to save his own skin.

Question 7. God intervenes to protect Sarah as he surely would have protected her husband.

Question 8. God's graciousness extends not only to the men he has chosen but also to the women.

Question 10. Abraham's actions raise several issues. First, the narrative answers the question of Ishmael's legal status; Abraham recognized him as a legitimate son (21:11; see 16:15; 17:23, 25, 26). Sarah's initial suggestion to have a son by Hagar recognized that he would be her own heir. She now fears that Ishmael would exercise his right of inheritance (v. 10). In accordance with current custom, she demands that Hagar and Ishmael be given their freedom and so renounce any claim to share the family estate. Abraham's distress is not over the legality of this action but expresses his fatherly love and concern. He acted because he was so instructed by God, who explained that Abraham's line will be continued through Isaac, yet Hagar and Ishmael will be cared for by God himself.

Study 13. Genesis 22—23. The Sacrifice of Isaac.

Purpose: To learn something of the way God provides for those who honor him with faith and obedience.

Question 1. Have volunteers for the roles of narrator, God, Abraham and Isaac read Genesis 22 aloud.

This narrative, which contains God's last recorded words to Abraham, is cast in the same literary mold as the initial call in chapter 12. It emphasizes the cost of the command, has a journey with unknown destination, separates the son from the father and ends with an altar, an offering and a promise.

Question 3. Note that the three-day journey requires ongoing trust and sustained obedience.

Hebrews 11:19 gives us additional insight into Abraham's response: "Abraham reasoned that God could raise the dead, and figuratively speaking, he did receive Isaac back from death."

The parallels between Abraham's sacrifice of Isaac and God's sacrifice of his own Son are numerous. In fact, Mount Moriah may have been visible to Jesus as he hung on the cross of Calvary. But for Jesus there was no last-minute reprieve.

Question 5. Fear of God means reverence and awe.

Question 10. This story is rich in the legal terminology found in Near Eastern court documents, including the detailed description of the property, presence of witnesses and actual use of the land to seal transference of ownership.

Question 11. As a resident alien, Abraham would have many rights, but not that of owning land. This episode is of historic importance as it marks the first actual possession of land in Canaan in Israel's history.

Study 14. Genesis 24:1—25:11. A Wife for Isaac.
Purpose: To look at the way God provided a wife for Isaac as an example of God's guidance and care in our lives.
Question 1. These last recorded words spoken by Abraham show the growth of his faith over the years. At the beginning he expressed doubt about the two most important elements of God's promise: his posterity (15:2) and the land (15:8). Now after years of struggle and testing, he reflects confidence that God will take care of what he has promised. He has become the exemplar of faith described in Hebrews 11:8-12, 17-19.

Placing a hand on the thigh (a symbol of the reproductive organs) when taking an oath in connection with the last wishes of a superior symbolizes an involvement of posterity in carrying out the instruction. It gives added solemnity to the obligation.
Question 2. Abraham's servant may be the Eliezer mentioned in 15:2. It might be well to note that the servant's prayer is uttered spontaneously, without formality. It shows an individual in direct contact with God, understanding that God is approachable and wants to help us.
Question 11. Significantly, this section of Genesis dealing with Abraham's death closes with genealogical lists detailing the patriarch's many descendants. They are a witness to God's faithfulness in fulfilling his promise that Abraham would be the father of many nations. His entire biography is enfolded in a framework of promise and fulfillment.

Study 15. Genesis 25:12—27:40. Jacob & Esau.
Purpose: To consider the powerful influence parents can have on children and family relationships. To think of ways to reduce family tension and encourage better relationships.
General note. This study covers two-and-a-half chapters, too long a narrative to discuss thoroughly. The questions are designed to help the group understand and apply the more important aspects of the lives of Isaac, Rebekah, Jacob and Esau without getting lost in the details.
Question 1. Note that when Rebekah was in distress, she had freedom to question God directly.
Question 3. The birthright was the status of the firstborn which bestowed headship of the family and a double share of the estate. Here this status has a special significance of both privilege and responsibility in continuing the line of Abraham and fulfilling the promises God made to him. Ancient documents show that among contemporary Hurrians the birthright was transferable, either by a decision of the father (see also Gen 49:3; 1 Chron 5:1) or purchase by another brother.

Question 6. If you think you have time, you may want to pick up the second part of 26 here and use the questions under "Now or Later."

Question 7. Ask volunteers for the roles of narrator, Isaac, Esau, Rebekah and Jacob to read 27:1-40.

Question 9. The biblical record doesn't condone Jacob's heartless exploitation of his brother's hunger and the crafty deception of his blind old father. The Lord's answer to Rebekah (25:23) makes it clear that Jacob's claim on the birthright is due solely to God's election. Furthermore, the next chapter will begin to show the painful consequences to Jacob for his cheating.

Study 16. Genesis 27:41—30:24. Jacob in Exile.

Purpose: To see how spiritual maturity often comes through suffering.

Group discussion. This is not designed to open up a gossip session. Characterize the family without tell-tale detail if others would know them.

Question 2. The title "God Almighty" *(El-Shaddai)* was specifically associated with the covenant with Abraham (17:1).

Question 4. The description in 28:12-13 resembles a typical Babylonian temple-tower, the ziggurat. But unlike the pagan version, on which the deity descends and the human ascends, angels use the stairway and God stands above it. This is the Lord's first self-revelation to Jacob, unexpected and undeserved but also unreserved in its blessing.

Question 5. Although Jacob's reply appears to be bargaining, it is more a pledge, following his awe and homage, to take the promise and act on it (v. 15). The offering of a tithe is not a gift but a giving back to God.

Question 7. Ask volunteers for the parts of narrator, Jacob, the shepherds and Laban to read chapter 29.

Question 10. The names of the babies in chapters 29 and 30 reveal the pathos and tension the two women experience in their momentary triumphs. The point of 30:14-16 lies in the fact that mandrakes were thought to induce fertility. Ironically, the man who bought the birthright from his brother is now bargained for by his wives. Although Leah was unloved, her sons Levi and Judah produced the most influential tribes in Israel, the priesthood and the monarchy.

Question 12. The narrative moves on two parallel tracks: God's mercy and providential care, and Jacob's moral responsibility and suffering the consequences of his sin. God reaffirms the covenant with Abraham and Isaac and gives specific promises to Jacob. Yet the home-loving Jacob is forced into flight, exiled from his family, ruthlessly exploited for twenty years and tormented by family tensions. Rebekah secures the birthright for her favorite son and succeeds in her strategy to save him from Esau by sending Jacob off with his father's blessing. Yet she does not bring Jacob back as planned but dies without seeing him again.

Study 17. Genesis 30:25—31:55. Jacob Versus Laban.

Purpose: To consider the consequences of unresolved conflict and how we can promote reconciliation in such relationships.

Question 2. The phrase *every speckled and spotted sheep* in verse 32 is absent from the early Greek translation of the Old Testament (the Septuagint) and may have been added later. Laban's action in verse 35 seems to confirm that Jacob's share consisted of the black sheep and speckled or spotted goats.

Question 4. This procedure with striped rods at breeding time was based on the mistaken belief that a vivid sight during conception leaves its mark on the embryo. Jacob also used selective breeding, a slow process, as Laban doubtless knew. So the only explanation for the rapid increase in Jacob's flocks is the miraculous power of God (see 31:10-12).

Question 5. Ask volunteers for the parts of narrator, Laban's sons, the Lord, Jacob, Rachel and Leah to read 31:1-21.

Question 6. Contemporary documents throw light on the women's statements in 31:14-15. Once married to Jacob they were considered outsiders and therefore could be subject to exploitation. The last sentence refers to the custom of the groom's depositing with the bride's father a sum of money to be settled on the bride after the wedding. Since Jacob's fourteen years of service was a substitute for money, apparently Laban had either failed to put aside the monetary equivalent or else used it for himself.

Rachel's theft of her father's household gods may have been motivated by the custom that their possession could strengthen a person's claim to the inheritance. It may also indicate her trust in God was not as strong as Jacob's.

Question 10. Fear of Isaac may be a way of identifying God as the object of Isaac's reverence and awe. Since the covenant feast was sacrificial, the parties would consider themselves bound together in the table-fellowship of their divine host.

Study 18. Genesis 32—33. Jacob Meets Esau.

Purpose: To consider the fact that much struggle is sometimes necessary to redress past wrongs and effect reconciliation with someone we have injured.

Question 5. Jacob's prayer is firmly grounded in God's covenant, command and promise. It has elements of fear and hope, gratitude, humility, confession, sense of vulnerability, and petition. Keep questioning the group to bring out some of these more important features.

Question 7. Here is a *theophany,* an "appearance of God" in human form. The Old Testament has numerous instances, beginning in Genesis 3:8, where God appeared to Adam and Eve in the garden.

Question 9. The name *Jacob* means "he deceives," and the name *Israel* means "he struggles with God."

The change of name portends a shift of emphasis from the individual to the people of Israel. This event marks a decisive break with the past and initiates

Jacob's new role as the father of the emerging nation. The place itself is significant since the river Jabbok is the boundary of Israel's first victory over the kings of the Promised Land. Jacob's decisive spiritual experience and change of name occur just as he crosses into the first territory to be occupied by the people of Israel as they emerge from the wilderness.

Joyce Baldwin comments on this event: "If God has forgiven his deception, as it seems he has done, Jacob could met Esau without fear. The sun rose upon him, and he was light of heart even though he had a permanent limp. His lifetime struggle against allowing the God of his fathers to hold the reins of his life had at last come to an end" (*The Message of Genesis 12—50* [Downers Grove, Ill.: InterVarsity Press, 1986], p. 138).

Question 10. Have volunteers for the roles of narrator, Esau and Jacob read chapter 33 aloud.

Question 12. Although Jacob told Esau he would join him in Seir (v. 14), he goes instead to Succoth then Shechem (vv. 16-20). His actions may indicate a reluctance to fully trust Esau in spite of their reconciliation.

Study 19. Genesis 34—36. Jacob's Compromise & Commitment.

Purpose: To consider the dangers and consequences of spiritual compromise or disobedience.

Group discussion. Watch your time, as the passage for the study is long.

Question 1. The city of Shechem is about a day's journey from Bethel and stands at a crossroads of trade.

Question 7. The fact that Jacob is named *Israel* again leaves no doubt that it is God who has changed his name.

Question 8. Bethel marks an end and a beginning for Jacob. It is a time of parting in the deaths of Deborah the nurse and his beloved wife Rachel. It is also a time of transition with the promises of God reaffirmed and the family completed by Benjamin's birth. From now on the focus shifts to Jacob's sons, whose descendants will become the twelve tribes of Israel.

Question 12. The brotherhood of Esau and Jacob remains prominent throughout the Old Testament in the nations of Edom and Israel. Chapter 36 traces in detail the descendants of Esau. As before, where a new stage of the narrative is about to begin, the genealogy of the other branch of the family is completed.

Part 3: Joseph—The Migration to Egypt
Study 20. Genesis 37—38. Joseph & His Brothers.

Purpose: To consider how even tragedy and evil can be part of God's plan for good.

Question 1. Have volunteers for the roles of narrator, Joseph, Jacob, the man, Reuben, Judah and the brothers read chapter 37 aloud.

Having the coat of many colors set Joseph apart and exempted him from the menial work of farming.

Question 3. Although God does not figure explicitly in these dreams, it is tacitly accepted that he is the source of the message. To show they are not simply idle occurrences, the dreams in Joseph's biography always come in pairs.

Question 4. Reuben has every reason to object to this plot. Blood, especially a brother's (4:10; 9:5), was sacrosanct. As the oldest brother he would be held responsible for it. Furthermore, he is already out of favor for sleeping with his father's wife. For him this is a make-or-break situation.

Question 5. A cistern is a kind of well that collects surface water during the winter rains but is empty during the dry season.

Question 6. Dothan was an important town on the ancient north-south caravan route. Slave trafficking was well-established by this time. Twenty shekels of silver equaled five years of wages for a shepherd.

Question 7. It is ironic that a goat should be chosen to deceive Jacob. (Recall how Jacob had deceived his father in Gen 27:9.)

Question 8. The biblical record gives unvarnished accounts of sinful actions and the way God uses them to achieve his purposes in human history.

Question 10. Since the Canaanites encouraged ritual sex as fertility magic, Tamar poses as a cult-prostitute. It is evident that Judah recognized Tamar's sons as continuing his line since Perez is listed in the genealogies of David (Ruth 4:18) and Joseph (Mt 1:3).

Study 21. Genesis 39—40. Slave & Prisoner.

Purpose: To consider Joseph's example of perseverance under pressure and the way he coped with shattering reverses.

Question 1. "The Lord was with Joseph" becomes almost a refrain together with the words "prosper" and "successful." Yet the blessing did not enable him to avoid trouble and testing. The injustice he suffered played its part in preparing him for the position of leadership he was to fill later in life.

Question 2. Joseph's moral standards should be appreciated against the background of sexual promiscuity that is characteristic of all slave societies. Unlike the ancient law codes of the Near East that treat adultery as an affront to the husband, the biblical view is that it is a sin against God. The standard of morality is not social but divine; therefore, it is not relative but absolute.

Question 4. An insult to the wife meant an insult to the husband.

Question 9. Have volunteers for the roles of narrator, Joseph, cupbearer and baker read aloud chapter 40.

Question 10. The chief cupbearer held the important office of trusted adviser to Pharaoh. The chief baker also had an important position since records list almost one hundred varieties of breads and cakes enjoyed by the Egyptians.

The biblical world recognized dreams as a vehicle of divine communication. They frequently produced anxiety since ignorance of a dream's meaning deprived a person of knowledge that might be vital to his welfare. Joseph's earlier dreams were immediately understood by himself and the family, but the cupbearer, baker and Pharaoh (chap. 41) needed an interpreter. Here is a crucial difference between biblical and pagan dreams: the latter developed professional interpreters and a dream literature. In the entire Bible only Joseph and Daniel interpret dreams. It is significant that each serves a pagan monarch in a land where dream interpretation flourished. Furthermore, both disclaim any innate ability and attribute the interpretation to God.

Study 22. Genesis 41—42. Joseph Governs Egypt.

Purpose: To see how adversity and disappointment can develop our character and prepare us to serve God more fully.

Question 3. Here we see both wisdom and discernment, gifts of God to his people in both the Old and New Testaments.

Question 4. The thirteen years Joseph spent in Egypt must have seemed endless, but during that time he rose from slave to second in the kingdom.

This narrative shows a remarkable degree of familiarity with Egyptian customs. Joseph's many titles and functions correspond with those found in ancient documents. The signet ring conveys Pharaoh's authority, the fine linen is court dress, the gold chain is a mark of royal appreciation, and the second chariot proclaims that Joseph is next to Pharaoh (vv. 42-43).

Question 8. Have volunteers for the roles of narrator, Jacob, Joseph, Reuben and the brothers read aloud chapter 42.

Twenty years have elapsed since Joseph's brothers sold him into slavery; he is now about thirty-seven.

Question 9. Joseph tests their honesty and is also able to find out what is happening to his family. By holding one brother hostage he can test whether they would trade him for food, as they had earlier traded Joseph for money.

Study 23. Genesis 43:1—45:15. Family Reconciliation.

Purpose: To reflect on those elements which are necessary to achieve reconciliation.

Question 1. At this point Joseph is about forty and Benjamin at least thirty years old. It was Judah who proposed that Joseph be sold into slavery.

Question 2. "God Almighty" (*El-Shaddai*) is a title specially connected with the covenant God made with Abraham and his descendants (Gen 17:1).

Question 5. The Egyptians' prejudice against eating with Hebrews was probably cultic since foreigners would technically defile the food. This attitude was evident later in Jewish refusal to eat with Gentiles.

Note in 43:28 the fulfillment of Joseph's boyhood dreams (Gen 37:6-11).

Question 6. Have volunteers for the parts of narrator, Joseph, the stewards,

Judah and the brothers read aloud chapter 44.

The drama now reaches its climax in the desperate situation carefully contrived by Joseph as a final test for his brothers. Since Joseph's silver cup has Egyptian religious significance (it is a divining goblet), its theft is all the more serious.

When Judah begs to take Benjamin's place, it is clear that the animosity between Rachel and Leah's sons is over. Jacob's sons would prefer Egyptian slavery to breaking their father's heart.

Question 9. Chapter 45 is the climax of the story of Joseph. It is a beautiful example of God's sovereignty.

Study 24. Genesis 45:16—47:31. Jacob in Egypt.
Purpose: To recognize that seemingly unrelated and perplexing events can fit into the tapestry of God's purposes for us.

Question 1. Note the realism and humor in 45:24 as Joseph sends his brothers off with the instruction, "Don't quarrel on the way!"

Question 3. Beersheba had been Isaac's center of worship.

In offering sacrifices to the God of his father Isaac, Jacob acknowledges the family calling and apparently is desiring permission to move out of Canaan. His attitude differs markedly from that of his grandfather Abraham in going to Egypt (Gen 12:10-20). This vision adds a new detail to the old promise at Bethel: the growth to nationhood will take place in Egypt (Gen 15:13).

Question 6. If you are short on time, you can summarize the genealogy in chapter 46, noting that the list of Jacob's family is arranged into the Leah and Rachel groups. Judah's family history has already appeared in chapter 38.

Question 7. Have volunteers for the roles of narrator, Israel, Joseph, Pharaoh and the five brothers read aloud 46:28—47:12.

Question 8. Egyptian antipathy toward shepherds is typical of town-dwellers' attitude to nomads. Joseph uses this antipathy to secure, with Pharaoh's blessing, this geographically isolated area to protect the family from the influence of mainstream Egyptian life. This isolation, combined with a belief that they would eventually return to Canaan, enabled Israel to maintain its national language, traditions and customs during the centuries of bondage.

Question 10. Modern readers tend to view Joseph's dealing with the hungry Egyptians as cruel exploitation. Why did he not give them food instead of demanding that they exchange herds, land and personal freedom for grain? In the ancient world it was regarded as an act of charity to buy the land of the destitute. Even taking them as slaves meant that they would be provided for during the rest of their lives. The positive Egyptian response to this action is revealed in 47:25.

Question 11. For an explanation of 47:29 see the note on question 1 of study 14.

Study 25. Genesis 48—49. Jacob's Blessing.
Purpose: To learn from Jacob the value of persevering in the life of faith.

Question 1. Have volunteers for the roles of narrator, Jacob and Joseph read aloud chapter 48.

Only in Joseph's case does Jacob accept his grandchildren as if they were his own sons. That they were born to an Egyptian mother is not regarded as any disqualification. When Jacob says, "They are mine," he is using an ancient formula for adoption.

Question 2. Jacob's blessing is from the God who is (1) the God of his ancestors, (2) his personal God who led him all his life long, (3) the God who appeared to him in three crisis points: at Bethel, Paddan-aram and Peniel.

Hebrews 11:21 selects Jacob's blessing of Ephraim and Manasseh as one of his most outstanding acts of faith. It also commends Jacob's faith in requesting that his body be carried back to Canaan for burial: "'Swear to me,' he said. Then Joseph swore to him, and Israel worshiped as he leaned on the top of his staff" (Gen 47:31).

Question 3. One aspect of Jacob's faith is seen in the names he uses to refer to God (48:15-16). "The God before whom my fathers Abraham and Isaac walked" (v. 15) recalls that the Lord steadied Jacob's faith in many crises (28:13-15; 32:9; 46:3). Jacob's long years as a shepherd described in 31:38-40 made him appreciate God's shepherding care for him (v. 15). The term *angel* (v. 16) recalls God's visible encounters with him at important turning points, especially at Peniel (32:22-32).

Question 5. This chapter records the last of great declarations of destiny in Genesis. The blessings and curses, promises and judgments, punctuate the narrative with a forward look to Israel in the Promised Land.

Question 6. This is a difficult question, and its answer has far-reaching implications. God not only forgives our past but redeems our future, conforming us to the image of his Son (Rom 8:28-30). Still we must wrestle with the consequences of past actions.

Question 7. It is from the line of Judah that Jesus the Messiah comes. *Judah* sounds like the Hebrew word for "praise."

Question 10. Jacob proclaims God to be the ruler of nature as well as history, even of "the deep" (49:25), the personified ocean and rival of the gods in pagan myths. "Mighty One" (49:24) describes God as the champion of Jacob and Joseph. "Almighty" (49:25) is used of God in connection with his covenant with Abraham, Isaac and Jacob.

Study 26. Genesis 50. Joseph's Final Years.

Purpose: To look at Joseph's example of forgiveness, love and hope.

Question 1. The burying place for the patriarchs continues to be prominent in the narrative. It represents the family's one remaining stake in the Promised Land, the only property it will own there for the next four centuries.

Question 3. This apparently fictitious story and the arms-length approach, in addition to his brothers' lack of trust in him, undoubtedly grieved Joseph.

Question 9. In Egypt 110 years was considered the ideal life span. This action was a further testimony to the Egyptian people that Joseph's commitment was to the true God.

Question 11. Often we hear that the God of the Old Testament is a God of judgment, whereas the New Testament (in the person of Jesus Christ) reveals a God of love and mercy. But throughout Genesis we have seen God's judgment coupled with his nurture, mercy and grace.

The patriarchal period both opens (12:2-3) and closes with the note of hope epitomized by Joseph's last words in verse 24. Genesis ends with the close of the formative period of Israel's history. In Exodus the great national drama begins to unfold.

Charles and Anne Hummel have extensive experience leading Bible study groups and training Bible study leaders. Charles is a former executive director of InterVarsity Christian Fellowship and past president of Barrington College (Rhode Island). He is the author of several books, including Freedom from Tyranny of the Urgent *and* Fire in the Fireplace *(both from InterVarsity Press). Charles and Anne are also the authors of the LifeBuilder Study* Spiritual Gifts.